Put Your Game Together

Ethical Management in Youth Sports and Business

Donnie Howell

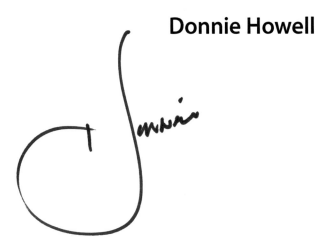

iUniverse, Inc.
Bloomington

Put Your Game Together
Ethical Management in Youth Sports and Business

iUniverse books may be ordered through booksellers or by contacting:

iUniverse
1663 Liberty Drive
Bloomington, IN 47403
www.iuniverse.com
1-800-Authors (1-800-288-4677)

Because of the dynamic nature of the Internet, any Web addresses or links contained in this book may have changed since publication and may no longer be valid. The views expressed in this work are solely those of the author and do not necessarily reflect the views of the publisher, and the publisher hereby disclaims any responsibility for them.

ISBN: 978-1-4401-9345-3 (sc)
ISBN: 978-1-4401-9347-7 (hc)
ISBN: 978-1-4401-9346-0 (e)

Library of Congress Control Number: 2009912369

Printed in the United States of America

iUniverse rev. date: 12/30/2011

About the Author

Born in Richmond, California, Donnie Howell is the kid who was raised on food stamps and little parental guidance. He discovered at a young age his needs would only be met through hard work and a game called football. In this book, Donnie puts together his story of childhood struggles and the lessons he learned along the way. A 1979 graduate of Pinole Valley High School in Northern California, Donnie received many high school football awards and achieved many accomplishments, such as setting the single-season record for quarterback sacks (twenty-five).

In 1993, he and his business partners started Bayview Environmental Services Inc., followed by Demo Masters Inc. in 2001. Combined, Bayview Environmental and Demo Masters employ over 200 people in what is now an employee-owned company.

Donnie has coached youth and high school football for twelve years, retiring in 2006. He incorporated the same ethics and principles as he did in managing and building these successful businesses. He has said, "If you want to get involved, then get involved with a passion to be fair to everyone and build a plan that proves it."

Along with his wife Leslie, the Howells now reside in Clayton, California, and vacation at their home in Rubicon Bay at Lake Tahoe, California, as much as they can.

Introduction

I believe that our kids, when signing up for a youth sport, are entitled to have fun. I believe that our kids have the right to a program that is built and designed by adults for their enjoyment. I also believe the parents and coaches are entitled to a good time as well. So why are our youth sports programs becoming such a mental drain to us, and why are our favorite pastimes becoming a burden?

I think good people are getting confused with winning and what winning really is about. We all want wins on the scoreboard and we all want the kids to have fun, but isn't winning also learning techniques, developing skills, building relationships, and creating a passion for the game and the smiles on kids' faces?

Building a winning program is not about building something just so it can win. It's about building something that creates winning character. Something everyone will buy into, and when they do, you and the people around you will be winners on the field and in life.

There are many stories in this book that will point out the many ways we need to focus on our own principles and ethics in order to build something fair. I also believe we need to judge ourselves before we start judging others. Look at your plan and ask yourself if it is as fair to everyone as I can make it and then ask yourself, can everyone be a part of it and will they? And when you have it, go and find people like you to help run it.

When given the opportunity you should surround yourselves with people who have the same ethics and principles as you do. Coaching youth sports or building a business requires the involvement of many people, and it will require you to spend many hours with them, so keep it as pleasant as you can. Recruit as many people as you can who will get the job done and instill your same ethical standards.

I played youth football as a kid and I really enjoyed it; while playing I met some great coaches as well as friends that I hang around even to this day. The memories are all pretty good as far as the coaching and my teammates are concerned. I also played in high school at Pinole Valley High under two coaching greats, Jerry Dueker and Jim Erickson along with their assistant coaches Butch Campbell, Mike Anton, and Fred Brown. These coaches are very special to me and I'll never forget them. They went out of their way to create fun for everyone, and they were winners too.

I have spent my twelve years doing my best to coach like they coached me. I've done my best to create a fun environment for the parents and the fans in our community as they did.

However, year after year, I could see things changing and coaches becoming more focused on "the scoreboard winning"; they were becoming more difficult to be around; and parents screamed from the stands at their own coaches. The young players have lost respect for the program and its coaching staff. What is going on and why?

This book will explain my thoughts on all this crazy madness and how we will fix it together and why we need more teams with good programs like Clayton Valley High and the new and improved Concord High Schools.

As a coach, I caught on to the teaching methods that Coach Deuker and Coach Erickson had in mind pretty fast. Although I found it through business.

While building the operations of my companies, Bayview Environmental and Demo Masters, I discovered the similarities. Coaching youth sports was very much like managing employees. We set out to build something fair and fun. We wanted our employees to enjoy work and we wanted employees who wanted to be challenged. Building a business is also developing relationships with the employees and clients. There are many ways you can bring in your life and business experiences into coaching. The tools are all around you if you want to build something enjoyable for everyone.

Build it the right way and you'll meet plenty of good people that will apply your standards as their own. Longtime relationships are nice to have.

I started coaching for Head Football Coach Herc Pardi at Clayton Valley High School in 1999. He was great to work with, and I still have some great memories there. My wife Leslie and I still spend plenty of good times with Coach and his wife Roxanne. We are together at parties and dinner outings as well as vacations at Lake Tahoe. I enjoy the time Coach and I spend talking about how things have changed since our playing days and how we still like being around the game. Discussing X's and O's is one of our favorite pastimes. Roxanne Pardi still performs by singing the National Anthem before some of the Clayton Valley High School football games. Leslie and I still enjoy going to watch the kids play football at the local high schools on Friday nights. Some of our favorites are Clayton Valley, Concord High, and San Ramon Valley, mostly because of our personal or family ties. We will even go to a Lake Tahoe Lakers game now and then, located in Lake Tahoe, California. Leslie and I have a cabin in Rubicon Bay and will drive the thirty minutes or so if they are playing at home on a Saturday. I will confess it's been a while since we have seen them play; I hope their program is doing well.

During my first year coaching at Clayton Valley, Coach Pardi asked me to be the defensive coordinator on the freshman team. I went over to meet with the freshman head coach, Sam Williams, and noticed he was working by himself, no other coaches in sight; he was coaching the entire team by himself.

I'll never forget that first day I went over to him and introduced myself. I said, "Hey, Coach. I'm Donnie Howell and I've been asked to help you with the team; I can see you could use some defensive help."

He said, "Yep. Good timing too. It's defensive day, and you're up."

"I don't understand," I said. "What do you want me to do?"

He responded, "It's defensive day. Tomorrow is offensive day. You're up."

I explained to him the only thing I could do with this short notice was what I've been working on at the youth level, and that was mostly form tackling, conditioning drills, and ball handling.

He said, "They need to know that too. Some of these kids are playing for the first time, and that is what I believe we should be doing anyway, you know, getting these kids ready to move up next year."

I liked what I was hearing. I have always enjoyed working with Sam, his ethics and his principles go unmatched, and the joy he gathered for himself when helping kids can never be compared. We have remained friends ever since that first day. He and his wife JoAnne have a son, also named Sam, who was drafted into the NFL by the Oakland Raiders.

Russ Galvin was and still is one of those guys you just have to love. This coach worked only for the kids and could care less what you thought about it. He wasn't one of those coaches who worried about the parents thinking he was a neat guy or anything like that. No, he just wanted the kids to learn proper football skills, and he wanted them to have a great time doing it.

Russ and I hit it off pretty well during our coaching years, and we had many of them.

We would sit around for hours after coaching youth football practices and just talk defensive football deep into some nights. His son Brock (who now plays football at U.C. Davis) would be at his side most of the time, saying, "Come on, Dad. I have school tomorrow. Can we go now?"

Russ and I were talking during one of our many nights after practice and I recalled him doing something earlier that day with one of the players. He was having a discussion with one of the kids, and I wanted to ask him what the talk was about. So I did. He said, "I always try to find a kid who is having some trouble and ask if I can help him. You see, things happen at home, and these kids get overlooked. I could tell his practice was way off from yesterday." As it turned out, the kid did have some minor problems at home. I found it really odd, you see, because I do the same thing and thought I saw it in Russ by the way he spoke to the kid. I knew right then this guy was true blue and he was in it for the right reasons.

I would find at least one kid every year who had some kind of home problems such as an abusive dad or a single-parent household, or who was a tough kid with a chip on his shoulder.

If I could help find one or two kids a year and get them and their families through the football season one day at a time and make it as fun as possible, then to me the season would be a winner, and that is what I also saw in Russ. He and Sam Williams are the kind of people who take pride in developing kids and players, so be selective when you have the chance to choose who will be around you and your athletes.

Building a business or a sports program starts with good knowledgeable people, the kind of people who have good ethics, good principles, and the desire to build something fair and fun for everyone.

Contents

Acknowledgments

Writing this book would never have happened had it not been for the persistent guidance and support of some very close friends like John Gregerson, Mike Peixoto, Mitch Larsen, Kristi Anderson, Steve Tuite, Gary Torretta, Jay Randall, Kurt Crigger, Tom Kennon, Sam Williams, Rick Cleveland, Michael Christie, Marvin Henderson, Pat Broderick, and Dennis Lee. To my brother Kevin, thanks for standing by me then and for standing by me now. I truly appreciate your never-ending support.

I also want to thank Nikki Crigger for reviewing and correcting the book. None of us would have ever understood what I was trying to say if not for her work.

Thank you as well to Mark McCullah for listening to me and taking my calls day after day whenever an idea came jumping into my head.

A special thank you to Russ Galvin, who told me to write this book for the benefit of others. His inspiration gave me the confidence to keep going. I hope I reached his level of passion to "do the right thing" in this book.

Thanks to my mother Barbara Lundquist; she's always in my corner and has always been my biggest fan.

Thanks to all the coaches I have worked for and with. I've enjoyed our friendships, and I'm thankful for the opportunities in coaching this great game. Thank you to Herc and Roxanne Pardi for your continued support and friendship.

Donnie Howell

Thanks to my sons Nick and Blake; I've enjoyed spending time with you guys both as a father and as a coach. But the biggest thank you is to my wife Leslie. Her unwavering love for me and the support she gives me with all of my crazy plans have helped me be the man I am today. We have been married for twenty-eight years, and she truly is my best friend. We got married at the ages of nineteen (her) and twenty (me) and have grown together happily ever since. We love our football seasons and we love our friends who do too. I also want to thank her for her part in making this a book that everyone should read.

1

Becoming a Winner

We all have hopes of being a successful person in the eyes of our peers and colleagues. Nobody sets out to be the coach who failed or the person who started a business that failed, so why do some fail? Because they are inconsistent with their decision making, they are not consistent in their principles, and they lack the courage to stay with their own created programs during the implementation period. They prefer to change in the direction of quick results rather than to ride out the learning curve.

The learning curve is extremely important because that is when it gets tested the most. If you allow yourself to alter or change your programs during the implementation period, then you are letting everyone involved with your programs know that with the right amount of pressure, you'll make changes to your programs from now on. Going forward, those programs are always challengeable.

As coaches, we want the parents to be proud of our work, and we would like the players to be proud of the program as well. Coaches generally feel they don't get enough credit or praise for the long hours they put into making a program great. In some cases, that is true. However, some coaches don't want to listen to others when it's obvious the program isn't working either. You don't hear them taking the blame for a program going badly, do you?

Let's stop worrying about credit and praise, and let's start worrying about taking some pride and ownership in what we are doing. Put pride on your side by doing the right things, and over time, you will get all the respect you can handle. If you don't have pride in the fact that you're doing the best job you can, and you haven't been dedicated and diligent in building a program that is designed to be fair to every single player, then you probably are not really working that hard at it and everyone knows it. If you are not 100 percent confident and proud of yourself, then why would you think someone else owes you compliments?

Let's start with being proud of what we are doing. Let's start with doing the right things the right way. Let's start by being committed to our principles and ethics. If you start with a mind-set for these things and you are committed to them for the duration of time, then you'll come out a winner, guaranteed.

Becoming a winner is not solely measured with victories. Victories are important and definitely make for a fun season, but you can also have a fun, successful season with everyone learning the game and competing. I'm all for winning games, just like anyone. Winning is more fun than losing; we all know that. The point here is that winning a game will not make you a winner. The victories will come, but that won't make you a winner. Winners have plans and winners stick to their plans because they believe in their plans, and soon others believe in their plans, and when that happens, they develop a team of believers.

You have to get respect from the players, and you have to get respect from the parents, and you have to get it because you're doing the right things.

You have been committed to the principles and ethics you set out to demonstrate. You have been thoughtful to the program and thoughtful to all the players involved, and you have stayed true to it over time. As your players and their parents see over time that you are committed to making kids better, and they see you take on challenges that come your way, over time, with consistency, they will start to learn what you are really about. I said "over time" because becoming a winner is just that: a long journey of consistent behavior, a long journey of decisions being made with good principles and ethics, tough decisions being made over time that are consistent with your beliefs, and staying true to your word and actions through good days and bad days.

Whether you have a firm personality or a meek personality doesn't matter. What matters is you are consistent with your decision making, and you constantly stay fair to the individuals involved. You don't waver on your programs because you put your principles and ethics into them already. You know what is best for everyone in the program because you thought about it and you employed the ideas from your coaching staff and your parents when you put it together. You asked everyone to get involved and be a part of the new program, and over time, they will be there for you.

So there is never a time when you will fold under pressure and be forced to make program alterations or changes. You won't be worried about that at all. You've been consistent, and you've stayed true to it over time. The only way time will hurt you is by not being true to your word; if you made up your programs that were not fair to everyone, if you built your programs in a half-hearted way and thought nobody else would notice, or if your programs had little thought and really did not apply to everyone, then most likely your plan will fail. Without putting enough time and thought into the program's potential downsides, someone could get missed and you will have problems to deal with. Mailing it in or not caring when program planning is concerned results in a program that will be full of holes, and you better be ready for some of those not-so-stupid people coming to you for explanations. They know you cannot explain your programs. They just saw you being inconsistent with other players. Don't make the mistake of thinking people won't know. It will follow you for many years.

Build your programs with good principles and ethics. Be fair to everyone when creating your programs. Short, tall, black, white, it doesn't matter. Just be fair to the programs you believe in, and stay consistent with them. I promise you'll end up a winner in the eyes of a lot of people. Take pride in what you are about to build.

Make it a statement of who you are and how you want people to feel about you because that is just what you are going to get.

Players need to work hard at becoming winners too. Just being a fast runner or great at throwing the ball will not make you a winner. If you are the kind of athlete who is constantly breaking the rules or taking time off during practice because you know you're one of the best players on the team, then you are really a distraction and a disappointment more than anything else. You will let your team down at some point. I can assure you of that. You will be the guy who will force a weaker coach into changing his programs to suit you. This will cause other players to challenge the system also, which will lead to weakening the team. The coaches will become overwhelmed with pressure from the parents, and they will lose interest in coaching. They will look to blame others, or they will look to blame the players. There is nothing good that will come out of a selfish player or a weak program.

If you are that great player, then embrace your coach's programs and try to be a role model for the younger players. With your God-given talent, why wouldn't you want to be in the best program you could be in? Why not embrace discipline for yourself and your coach's programs? Working hard at your talent and working hard at getting good grades could get you a scholarship to college, but being a good teammate and being a good role model will make you a winner in the real game: life.

Our elected officials and our school administrators have a big role to play here as well. They also need to set standards for these programs to follow. They need to have programs in place to save our school sports programs. They need to provide programs to help with fundraisers to keep these programs active. They need to have a good program in place for hiring head coaches. They need to use good principles and ethics when developing their programs, just as we all do. These elected officials and our school administrators should have a program in place that will work closely with their school sports programs. They should be working closely with the Booster Clubs, and they should be listening to the parents as problems or concerns take place. They should follow up on complaints from parents and not just disregard them as if the parents simply made it up. Take some action and do some interviews from both sides; if nothing else, your coaches and parents will know you have a plan and a system in place that will work for everyone. There should also be programs in place to remove coaches who are not positive role models for our kids. So many times you see a sports program getting worse and worse as years go by. It never gets better because the same lousy head coach is still there coaching year after year. This is a problem that nobody wants, and it is a problem that has to change. After a period of time, the kids will start believing in losing and believing that they will never be winners. They will become too embarrassed to play for the school and stop playing sports. Then it could be on to drugs or becoming an uninterested student.

If you're an elected official or a school administrator, this is your chance to be a winner too. Why not develop your programs to help kids stay in sports, and why not have standards for coaches to follow when dealing with our athletes? With your help and with the coaches teaching the right things, everyone wins. When you're getting out there in front of the parents and they're seeing you participate in the betterment of the programs that are designed for their most prized possessions, their kids, they'll be very grateful and support you.

The athletes will learn lessons from the communities that you're building for them. They will become long-term players and supporters in the community themselves, such as business owners, coaches, congressmen, and community organizers. There are too many cities these days across America that have kids in them that cannot wait until they are eighteen years old so they can move out of their hometowns and start a life somewhere else, and to me that is sad; keep your kids home. Build them a community filled with activities and sports programs and make it fun and fair for everyone.

If the elected officials and the school administrators took some responsibility, we could get our sports programs back in shape. We would have programs with funding, and we would have kids who would be proud to participate in them. We would have a community that is full of elected officials and administrators who are all winners. You'll see it in the next elections because they will all come out winners.

Parents can be a distraction or they can be a big help. Which are you? The parents' role in youth and high school sports is to be supportive to the program. The parents should be willing to help when asked and should be dedicated to supporting their kids. They should also be policing the program in order to help keep the program going in the direction that was lined out from the beginning. In order for the parents to be winners, they too need to fulfill their duties and know their places. A big part of a successful program is having all the kids ready to play.

Parents need to be sure their kids are staying up with their grades, make sure their kids are attending school, make sure their kids are getting support and praise, and make sure their kids are supportive and respectful to the program. The parents also have a duty to report to the head coach when a program is not operating in the way it was described. The parents need to become vocal to administrators and elected officials should any program disputes reach a level that cannot be worked out between the parents and the head coach. Parents helping the program and not trying to run the program is what I'm saying here.

I don't want parents thinking they're in charge of the program. No, that's the head coach's job. But if parents fully understand the program description that was laid out by the head coach, then they have a duty to discuss it with the head coach. If the parents feel that the program is failing to stay on the course that was presented to them, then you bet I want them to have a discussion with the head coach and explain their position on the matter. Both the parent and the head coach are adults, and they should both know that communication is king, so I do believe respectful dialog between them is a good thing because they both should want what is right for the kids.

By trying to be supportive of a head coach's program and by asking to be a part of the head coach's program, the parents will be a welcomed part of the team's success, and everyone will come out winners. The ultimate team approach to winning is everyone's involvement. Everyone being supportive and everyone being a part of the plan is success for everyone to enjoy.

Knowing why you want to be a coach in the first place is important. It is just as important as knowing why you want your kids to even play the game. It goes for an elected official, and it goes for a school administrator. Why are you in this profession in the first place? If you are in it and you want your kids in it, don't you want to do it right? Don't you want yourself and everyone around you to be successful? Of course you do.

I coached with a guy who once told me that his biggest dream was to be a head coach and to be a physical education (P.E.) teacher at a high school. A year later, he had his dream come true. After several years of disappointments from parents, players, assistant coaches, and himself, he told me he wanted to go and coach somewhere else. I asked him why he felt he needed to go and coach somewhere else. He said because he had learned some lessons and would like to get a fresh start. He would do things differently this time. I said to him, "You once told me that all you ever wanted to be was a head football coach and a P.E. teacher. You now have your wish, so why are you letting yourself be a horrible head football coach and a horrible P.E. teacher? You don't have to leave here to be better. You just have to realize you've achieved something special, and you need to appreciate it and have respect by doing it right." I also told him he could change right here, right now. People will forgive and forget if you are sincere about changing for the better. It's never too late to come out a winner.

One of the reasons I wrote this book was because running a business, in many ways, is just like coaching football. Replace the players with employees or replace parents with clients. Perhaps change assistant coaches with coworkers and administrators with building owners. It is all interchangeable to me. You can be a winner in both. As a matter of fact, I'm sure if you are a winner in one, you will be a winner in the other. I'm also just as sure that if you fail in one, you're likely to fail in the other too.

Principles and ethics play a large role in the outcome of any successful person. To me, there are two types of people who become successful: One learns lessons along the way through trial and error. This successful person doesn't repeat his mistakes too often. This person gets smarter, and he gets more confident as time goes on. He also learns to keep his ideas and lessons to himself in hopes of staying successful. The other type of successful person also learned some lessons through trial and error and became smarter as time went on, much like the first successful person. However, this successful person wants to teach his lessons learned from trial and error to others in hopes of teaching them to become successful in a more efficient way.

People who can believe enough in themselves to teach others are people who believe they will never be less than great. Those are the kinds of people who will always be winners. They don't fake it, and they don't mail it in. They are not intimidated about starting over or being replaced. They are not worried that you will not like them or that you will hate their programs. They are not worried about a parent supervising one of their practices. They are not worried because they know they are doing it the right way, and they know the right way has never been wrong.

Trust yourself and keep doing what your heart tells you to do. Knowing right from wrong doesn't come from a book. It's already built in you. Keep making people happy, and over time, you'll come out a winner.

If you haven't done it yet and you plan on changing your programs to include your good principles and ethics and you plan on bringing your coaching staff and parents together, then let me be the first to congratulate you on your future success. Stick with it, and over time, you'll become a winner.

2

Building the Right Base

Coaching and business are very similar in many ways because they work hand in hand with doing the right things and by making decisions through thoughtful insight. You would not make a decision to send your quarterback out onto the field without your offensive linemen, any more than you would send your foreman into an asbestos-filled building without proper training, protective clothing, and a respirator, now, would you? Of course not. Coaching is just like a business because when you start up a team, you need to get it going with the same principles that you would use in starting a business. You have to have a base to start with, one that is strong and consistent, and you will need principles and philosophies with sound rules. You need to lay everything out for everyone to see and follow. Things like a successful game plan, philosophies, and rules; evaluating risk; managing players; marketing creatively; teaching safety, punishment, praise, goals, and life's lessons; and so on.

A successful game plan in business is a plan on how to succeed in your marketplace and how you measure up to the competition; you review your staff and supporting team, you make changes in personnel if necessary, and you review and look over your equipment to see if it is adequate to accomplish your plan. You

---

make changes if needed, you replace equipment if it's not getting the job done, and you manage the current staff you have or make changes in this area in order to be competitive for the up-and-coming year.

A successful game plan in football is a plan in which you evaluate the coaching staff and players that you have for this season, you assess what type of offense or defense you can run based on the level of talent you have with the coaches and players, you review the condition of your practice equipment, and you spend time with the supporting staff and gauge their abilities to assist you. You make changes as you see fit to continue the plan, or you reevaluate the plan. These are the same things that need to be done whether you're building the base for a business or coaching a team.

You need to spend quality time with your coaches and teach them your philosophies every day. These coaches need to know who you are. They will believe in your message the more they are around you if you are always speaking the same message. This message is always spoken because you believe in it, and it should be a message that is right for everyone and easy to follow. A message that is inconsistent or is constantly being misrepresented is one that's hard for anyone to follow. You need a good message, one that is about fair play, safety first for the kids, teaching the sport, practicing to win, the rewards of working hard, consistency, keeping up with your grades, treating everyone fairly and respectfully, respecting authority, and working fairly with everyone. Who is not going to follow those examples? I'll say it's someone who is not like me, that much I know.

If you stick to your core beliefs, ethics, and philosophies, and these are as fair to everyone as you can make them, then people will follow without question. Your coaches will want to follow because it's something good, and they will become part of it. They will take on your philosophies as if they were their own, and your players will learn to adapt. The parents will know where everyone stands and what their roles are. It is very important to lay these rules and philosophies out for all to hear, starting on the first day.

If a player has failing grades and your system in place is serious about the kids maintaining good grades, then everyone will understand from the beginning what will be in store for this kid. You already laid it out for everyone to understand from the beginning. The kid will either stay at home with his parents until the grades start to show improvement or sit in the bleachers with a tutor until the grades start to show improvement. This is what you said would happen on the first day, so nobody will assume that this kid is going to be allowed to practice or play in any games because that was explained from the very beginning and this was understood up front by everyone. The kid knows, the parents know, and your coaches know. The rule was grades first, and it doesn't matter if this kid is the third-string center or the first-string quarterback. It's your school grades first and then the privilege of playing with your teammates. Getting the assistant coaches, parents, players, and even the football booster committee to know what your rules are and how they get handled from the very start is so important.

The next most important thing is sticking to it. So don't make up rules that you cannot or will not keep. Don't make up rules or punishments that you can't or won't stick to. If a player shows up late for practice, you may say, "You're late, and you can't practice for a week, and you won't play in next week's game." Then the player's dad hears about your punishment and thinks it's okay to plead a case for his kid. He tells you that your rule is a little ridiculous and maybe a warning would be better this time. Well, you agree that the punishment was too harsh, and you give the kid a warning and let the kid come back to practice and play in the next game. What kind of message are you sending now? The parents will question everything you do from then on, and the coaches will have a hard time following any message or philosophies you may have had because they don't see or hear you on a consistent basis doing the same thing. You just can't make up policies that you don't believe in yourself. If you can't follow your own rules, then why would you think someone else would? Lay out your thought-out rules from day one and stick to them. Over time, they will become automatic for everyone.

Your base should also include spending time developing players with safety in mind. When you think of conditioning and hitting drills, you should also think about water and hydrating the kids and coaches. Make sure you have plenty of coaches or parents with CPR and first aid training at practice. Most coaches think about CPR and first aid trainers and water on game day but don't realize that more kids get heat stroke or hurt at practice than in a game.

Tackling drills are not for the coaches to get a kick out of watching the bigger kids rip on the smaller kids. That is unsafe and usually not fun for the smaller kids, plus that should be a sign to you that these coaches have no idea what they are doing. If they think this is neat, then you better go over there and question their reasoning for coaching in the first place. You as the head coach or assistant coach should be involved with the drills and insist on making good decisions about who is to run the drills and making sure the coaches know that tackling drills are to teach the kids proper angles, keeping their head in an upward position, coming in low, wrapping up, and driving high. The kids should be sized up to be as equal as possible for the purpose of safety and physically being able to learn the drill correctly. Once in a game or scrimmage, they will be tackling kids of a larger and stronger size, yet they will be better prepared to handle what's coming with proper technique and skill.

The same thing goes for a business. You need to take into consideration the weather and the type of work that is going to be performed that day and think of anything that might go wrong and get a plan to prevent it and protect everyone from danger. A coach is kind of like a project superintendent. They are the ones we look up to. They have the experience and the knowledge to make the project work. They are also the ones who have to think before the others and assume the responsibilities of it.

Safety in the workplace or on a football field is not something to be taken lightly or something that you just pass on to someone else to worry about. No, it is in everyone's best interest to have a stake in it.

Tackling drills, sprints, get-offs, and scrimmages are all things that need a safety plan. When taught right, this game of football can be a lot less violent. Hard hitting is the game of football; however, teaching how to take a hit and how to give a hit the proper way is the responsibility of the coaches. And once taught correctly, you will have a group of players who are ready to play hard and safely.

Part of your business and football team base is creative marketing. What? We know what this is in business. It's doing something a little differently from the normal type of advertising of your company and differently from what your competitors have been doing for years. Creative marketing in business is more like sending out postcards with an offer to check your Web site for the opportunity to win a free lunch for your entire office. This works and has good intentions because you really do have something you want to offer. You want to build your customer base back up during tough times, and you want to separate your name from the competition.

Creative marketing in coaching is no different than in business because you are working hard to keep the kids interested in coming back next year. If they are not having a good time and their parents dislike the program, then they will not come back the following year. Your creative marketing is not on a postcard. It's in your coaching, it's in your philosophies, it's in your rules, and it's in your knowledge of the game and how you treat people. Sure, some kids will come back because their dads played the game and their kid will too, no matter what. Some companies will still use your services because the owner of their company knows the owner of yours. But you as a coach want to put your best effort out there every year to keep kids interested, so you really are marketing yourself and your program. If you're coaching in high school, you may also need to raise money; you'll need to market for that as well.

Once you build the base, the rest will work. It will start to take the lead without you spending much time on it. The marketing is being done every day, like dealing with the kid with the bad grades. Everyone knows up front what is going on because you explained it in the beginning, and as it continues with consistency in the right direction, it grows stronger and stronger.

Punishments are no different. They, too, need to be consistent and fair. Everyone gets the same punishment for the same faulty act. A punishable act is not to be set up in a manner that you find yourself unable to maintain it or remain fair about it. It has to be equal to all players. I shouldn't have to explain this, but I did coach for twelve years and have seen some pretty crazy stuff.

The act that was broken is the act with the punishment. Meaning if a player gave a cheap shot to a kid yesterday and you, the coach, made him run a mile and return to practice, then if another kid who you really don't like that much does the same thing today and you make him take off his pads, leave the field, and hit the showers, then this would be inconsistent punishment, which would jeopardize the integrity of your program's base. When you have these types of inconsistencies in your program, you leave the door open for a coach, a parent, or a kid to question and negotiate your decisions. You will find yourself spending more time explaining your decision making than you will building your program.

The same thing will apply in the working world. Instead of setting the focus on moving forward, you will find yourself going backward explaining and changing the negative parts of your plan. How much time do you want to spend on punishment anyway? Be consistent. Have a punishment plan in place to move the program or company forward, and stick to it no matter who made the mistake. Only then will your base plan start to get a life of its own. Everyone will understand the base needs punishments to keep people focused on growth and staying on track; they won't understand a leader who thinks he or she can bully people around with their authority and have different punishments for different people. Besides, in case you were ever to be sued, you had better have a documented plan that is consistent and fair to everyone.

I've seen where some coaches punish players for being hurt. They call them the "Kaiser Crew" or the "Walking Wounded." Now, don't misunderstand me here. I do know some kids try to get out of practice by pretending to be hurt, but do you really care? Most kids who pretend to be hurt are not great players anyway. These kids are not having fun either, so let them be. Spend your time and focus on the kids who want to learn. I don't understand it when a coach punishes a kid who has a bad back. This kid will have to go around the practice field and pick up trash in an attempt to make him want to come back and practice. This kid has a note from his doctor saying he cannot practice, and the coach decides he needs to pick up trash, bending over with a bad back to pick up trash, in an attempt to make him want to come back and practice with his teammates. Here are two thoughts on this, and believe me, I don't know why this needs to be said either, but #1. He might really be hurt, and the coach telling him to pick up trash is only going to make his back worse and prolong the recovery. #2. If the coach would be more creative with practice and made it educational and fun, then nobody would want to miss it anyway.

As a coach or business professional, you are also liable for the decisions you make in regard to someone else's personal well-being. Why on earth would you think you know more than the kid's doctor, and why would you voluntarily stick the liability foot in your mouth? Just focus on the kids who can and want to play.

During one of my youth football coaching days, I was taking over for the head coach who could not make practice. We started with some stretching and moved through our get-offs and quick, short sprints, then broke into our groups: running backs with running backs, which is where I was, receivers with quarterbacks and receivers, linemen with linemen, and so on. About twenty minutes later, we had a water break, and I looked at one of the kids who came from the linemen drills. His face was striped with blood, like an Indian warrior. I asked him what had happened, and he told me he had a bloody nose. His coach told him to rub it all over his face, and that would make him look tougher. I almost flipped my lid. I went over to the coach, who, by the way, was a registered nurse, and said, "What the heck, man? You of all people should know better than that. What were you thinking? Kidding around or not, that was stupid."

He responded by saying it wasn't that big of a deal and this little trick stopped the player from crying.

"Did you think about spreading germs around or something worse to the other kids?" I said.

"No, not really," he replied.

As it turned out, it was not that big of a deal, but coaches, especially at the youth and high school levels, must remember that these kids are loved and adored by their parents too, just like you adore yours. You have an obligation to treat them all as if they were yours and make decisions based on that thought. Some of those kids may not be the best athletes or may not be the hardest workers, but they are loved by someone very much and deserve to be treated that way. You will not always be coaching at a level that your kid is playing, and you will want to know your child is in the hands of someone who is doing the right thing and has a base plan for success. Some of these kids may not be productive on a football field, but they may be a future president of a bank, or run a clothing franchise, or who knows what else? Don't underestimate what they may become.

Your base plan should have these and many more items addressed prior to anything else at your first day's meeting with the coaches, parents, and players. You must be the kind of person who has good ethics and principles and is a thinker, or you need to step aside and let the people who want to do the right thing take over. Start with your base plan and surround yourself with people like you. Instill your ethics and principles, and you'll be greater than you could imagine.

Remember, understand your own base, explain it to everyone up front, stick to it as fairly and consistently as you can, and you'll have a great time. You will be well liked and respected, and the winning will come whether you are in business or coaching.

3

Getting with Your Plan

Some of the youth football coaches I worked with or have been around would come out coaching the very same way every year, never to learn from the year before or bring something new that they may have learned at a football clinic (probably because they never went to one) to make the new year a fun one. They would start every practice with the kids running a marathon. Yep, practice would be something like this every day: The whistle blows and it's a marathon run, one to two miles. After that, run up and down the bleachers. Line all the kids up for jumping jacks, sit-ups, push-ups, leg lifts, and then run a mini-marathon again. Break into ball-handling drills for the running backs, pad-hitting drills for the linemen, tackling drills for the linebackers, and so on, then scrimmage and scrimmage and scrimmage, then run another mini-marathon and call it a day.

I would like to see coaches in the off-season work on a plan for a better way to teach kids more about the game of football, fundamentals of the game, tackling skills, position play, and technique, things like this. I believe coaches should make practice fun. You can work hard on getting what you want out of practice, but take the time to make it where the kids want to come back, and not just next year. I'm talking about tomorrow and the next day.

Use simulation drills. This was my favorite part of practice. I would watch my position players during practice and during games, in this case the running backs, and see what they were doing after they took the ball and think of a drill that would simulate what was going on out there on the field during play, proper ball control, reading levels, power running, cutbacks, blocking, things like this, and then reenact it all with simulation drills. Work them through it and watch them get better. This also breaks up practices by not doing the same drill all year long. Some drills have to stay in because they are equally important. However, the kids love to learn, and you need to find a way to hold their attention while you are helping them learn a new skill.

During the off-season, a coach can go online and buy DVDs on fundamental drills or practice drills for each position. Have a plan. The kids don't need to run a marathon to start practice, so you can burn up some time. If you don't have enough drills to teach the kids, buy a tape or a DVD, and don't be afraid to learn. Football is a quick, speed game. Nobody runs for much more than a hundred yards at any one time. Work on stretching, sprints, and get-offs. There is just no excuse not to have a plan. Ask your coaches to buy tapes that relate to the position that they will be coaching. If you plan to be a head coach for a long time, you may consider buying a series of tapes you like and lend them out to your coaches. This way, you will be able to see that they are coaching what you want them to, and it will allow you to step in and replace a coach should one not be able to make a practice or two.

The Concord High School football team was not very good before we took the program over. Every one of us had good intentions when we took on the responsibilities of this team and its community. Myself as the assistant head coach and running backs coach met with the new head football coach, the offensive coordinator, the defensive coordinator, and a few of the assistant coaches to discuss our plan. Our plan was simple and direct, to the point. We wanted to bring pride back to the community. We all understood that this community had been given a bad rap because of the football program that they had before. The kids and the parents welcomed us. This group of parents already knew about most of us. Russ Galvin was very well respected for his work with his church and with the youth and high school football teams in our neighboring town of Clayton, California. They also knew Mark McCullah as a Clayton Valley High football coach and community supporter for the city of Clayton. The most well-known, I'm sure, was my wife Leslie, for her endless work and support for Clayton Valley High School and youth sports, and of course, myself for some of these same reasons. Some of the kids and parents knew us from youth football because kids in the neighboring cities, Concord and Clayton, would play for one or the other youth football programs.

The new Concord head coach and the coordinators also developed very good standings with the community from their coaching work at Clayton Valley High School as assistant coaches. With the head coach and the people he was bringing to the program, this town was looking toward a great football season, at least on paper.

The plan was going pretty well the first year. We had parent involvement and support. The head coach and I would attend the Booster Club meetings. Concord's Booster Club people were great. They got a new field, new lights, new bleachers, and fencing through their hard work. We coaches even had plans to develop a new snack shack. The head coach put together some great ideas with new uniforms and helmets and one of the best weight room workout programs in the area. Everything was going pretty well. Parents were happy, assistant coaches attended meetings, and they also showed up at night in the weight room to help out. I was on top of our plan to make this program better and would be there to reel in someone should they start getting ideas that we never discussed.

Then we started coaching, and the short-term success was getting in some heads. Coordinators were not working with their assistants, which caused some tension. Some parents had problems with the way their kids were being treated by the coaching staff. The head coach was having a problem with a few parents. He could not understand how they could have a problem with him. He did not handle these types of problems very well. He and the coordinators were pretty young and needed to grow up a little.

You see, a well-thought-out plan is a must. The plan needs to have strength, it needs to be bigger than those who developed it, and it needs to be a good moving plan. These young coaches had a lot of potential in being really good coaches and doing the right thing for the community, and they committed to bring back its pride. However the early pressure to win got in their heads.

The problem with a plan is keeping it in place above everything else, even winning. When you start up a program or take one over, you have to be committed to it. It's your base for what you believe in. Winning will come once you get everyone dedicated to the plan. If you let parents, administrators, fans, or boosters apply pressure on you to win, and that pressure allows you to move away from your plan, then either you must have built a plan you don't believe in or you're coaching for the wrong reasons.

The plan should be built with respect for winning and put into place to teach your kids the fundamentals of this game and the fundamentals of life. If you put those things in your plan and allow somebody to put enough pressure on you to change it, find something else to do. Get your plan in place before you start. Make it something that you really want to accomplish, and nobody will move you from it.

President George W. Bush had his plan when he was in office, and to some, it did not work. The point here is he has gone home to Texas with his head held up high, knowing he did what he believed was right for the plan, and nobody gave him a good enough reason to change it.

You may find you did not win all the games you set out to win your first year or two, but you won't be a loser, either. Winning comes with the plan. If you plan to build a program or take one over, you must have your plan in place and stick to it. In the early years, don't worry so much about winning or losing, worry more about who stayed within the plan and who did not. These are the coaches, parents, or players who are going to help the program down the road. You cannot deviate from your plan, either. Come on. Who will follow something you set up and won't follow yourself? A plan can be altered to better serve your needs, but don't fool yourself into taking a shortcut, because there is no shortcut in doing the right thing.

This is when you know your plan is starting to take over: The incoming kids and their parents learn from the ones who have been with you, and they explain to the incoming kids and their parents that this is the plan to play here. They believe it because you are living it also. Even the hotshot kid who is in some kind of trouble will learn fast if you stick to the plan, he sees you benching or punishing another great player, and you are not showing favoritism. The football team has no room for the ones who don't practice hard, don't keep up with their grades, or disrespect a coach or a teammate. The plan will grow and take a life of its own, and after a couple of years, it will become the program.

To the credit of the Concord head coach, he did grow up a little. He found his plan and has made some really nice progress there. As for the Concord community, they never really needed our help anyway. They were born with pride and still have plenty of it.

When I was growing up, my siblings and I had no money, and there was not much we could do about it either. We were too young to work legally, except for my older sister. But even then, my brother Kevin and I had to come up with a plan. We could not keep going without one. We needed money for school clothes and other essentials. I think we were born with the thought of having to have a plan. Kevin is thirteen months older than I am, and we are very close because of our closeness in age and our early-on common struggles.

When we were eleven and twelve, we were living in San Pablo, California, which is not the greatest place in the world, but we survived. A friend of Kevin's found a job selling candy to office people. They would meet some guy who had boxes and boxes of candy (almond cluster type) in his van. It was summertime, and school was getting close. Neither Kevin nor I had anything to wear for the up-and-coming school year. This friend of his asked us if we wanted to sell the candy too. We, of course, jumped all over the idea. Work? You bet. We would meet this guy in front of Long's Drugstore, sign out for our boxes of candy, and get on a bus to Oakland, which was about twenty miles away. It was a long day doing this little job, but I thank God for finding it for us and for getting us a plan, for that year anyway.

This working thing started something for Kevin and me. We knew we had to have a plan every summer, and we did. Mowing lawns, painting fences, a paper route, working at whatever we could do. We understood that work is what we needed to do to help with the family and for us to have a chance to prosper as well. We never took to stealing or crime. Any weak person can come up with that plan, but no, not Kevin and me. We had our plan, and it was to work hard and give someone a reason to want us back.

With the economy in the condition that it is in today, I'm recommending to the young adults who are between the ages of eighteen and twenty-five to get with their plan. A lot of these young people had everything they needed while growing up. When they were eleven or twelve, they got it all just by asking. They didn't even need to work it off. They didn't have to do yard work, and they didn't have to help out in the kitchen. They just got it because Mom and Dad had it. There was no demand for them to do chores. Mom had a housekeeper who came once a week, and Dad had a gardener for the yard on Saturdays. As long as these young adults stayed out of trouble and worked on their schooling, they would get whatever they wanted. The average family had plenty to give them. Their parents were making really good money, and they were very comfortable.

Their parents had more money than their parents ever had and felt bad if they told the kids "no" when the kids asked for something. These parents knew what that feeling was like from when their parents said "no" to them. These parents knew they could afford it and would give in the next day after another request. At no fault of their own, these young adults simply got whatever they wanted.

Things are changing big time now, with some of these parents getting laid off or experiencing compensation cutbacks, no more bonuses, no more car allowances, and buying less at Christmastime and birthdays for these kids. Now these young men and women have some major adjustments to make, and nobody is offering them a class on it, except for me: "Get with Your Plan."

Young men and women need to start thinking about a plan that will help them grow into functional adults. They need to start with a short-term plan about focusing on completing college, if they are still going, and if not, getting to work now, any kind of work that they can do that will help them get a paycheck and some independence. Make arrangements to live with their parents, and start saving some money. If that is not an option, then get a place with a friend or get their own place, whatever will do, or whatever they can afford.

These young adults need to start asking themselves what they want to become and start setting some goals. With a plan, things will become reachable and not so depressing. These can be happy times, with pride and purpose. They will start to understand how great independence and supporting yourself can be. They will start to appreciate why you, their parents, so badly could not wait to be an adult. With direction and a plan, they too will become successful adults. Everyone needs a plan: high school football athletes, coaches, employees, supervisors, parents, and business owners as well.

They should take the time to evaluate themselves and put their plan into action with reachable goals. Once they accomplish a goal, then set up another, then another. It also goes for you of any age. Set your own goals and enjoy your personal growth. With a plan, these young adults will overcome the handouts we so lovingly gave them.

A final thought on the plan: It must be monitored and altered as things change. This is normal and should be addressed with thought and using your ethics and beliefs. Keep to the core of the plan, work hard at it, treat people right, and good things will come your way. I believe we all get plenty of opportunities for change, but it's only the people who are looking to change who are really the ones who will ever see it. Keep an eye out for yours.

I was twenty-five years old and working in a machine shop back in early 1986. I was doing pretty well there as far as work is concerned but wasn't getting a feeling that this type of work was right for me. It was the beginning of my third year there, and I had come to the conclusion that working in the machine shop wasn't for me at all. I had enough. I just could not believe that my life was to be spent going to the same building every day, listening to the same coworkers talking about the same thing every day. God bless them. They meant no harm, but I was ready to put my head into one of the machines if I heard one more time from my coworker that he was upset about his messed-up wife or the lady running the drill press showed me a picture of her grandchild again. You spend all of your time with the same people eating lunch, having a coffee break, and talking crap about other people. You and your people talk crap about the other people's groups that decided to form a crap-talking group of their own without your approval. It is unbelievable what happens to you between those concrete walls. The worst part is you miss these people when they are not at work. If they don't show up one day, you start to ask yourself questions like, "Who is going to hear about my same crap today? When is he coming back? Is he sick? Did his dad die? We were talking about the same old crap yesterday, and he never mentioned he was not going to be here today. What's up with that?" I started to get a little crazy.

I needed to get myself out of there and back on track. This was not for me, and I needed a better plan. The problem here was I had a two-year-old son, a wife, a house payment, good pay, and really good benefits. Stuck, I guess.

A few months later, a very good friend of mine was working at this insulation company. He was doing really well there and was moving up fast. He told me the company was looking to hire some quality people and wanted to know if he could give out my name.

I said, "What does it pay?"

"I'm not sure," he said, but he was making more than I was at the time, so it must be good.

"Thanks," I said. "I will talk it over with Leslie and get back to you soon."

After discussing it with Leslie, I was ready for the move. God knows I was ready. I met with one of the owners and was feeling good about our interview, and then the big question came up. I asked him, "What does the job pay?"

He said, "$12.00 per hour."

I said, "Wait a second here. I'm making more than that at my other place. I can't work for that. I have a kid and a house."

He understood and really wanted me there, and I wanted to be there, but his problem was no one else who was not a foreman was making what I did at the machine shop. So, I quickly came up with a plan. I said to him, "If you really want me here, then let's make a deal. I will work for the $12.00 per hour for three months. After that, I get moved up to foreman level and run my own projects."

He said, "What if you're not ready?"

I said, "Don't worry. I'll be ready because you are going to put me with your best foreman."

He laughed and said, "Deal."

I did not want him to put me with my friend because I did not want to put any burden on my buddy, since he was moving up to be the company's first superintendent, and he needed to learn his own new job.

Things did not run very well with this company at first, and it really was not the fault of the owners entirely. The owners were committed to being a good company. They spent time trying to find better foremen and laborers. They paid the good people pretty well in hopes to make the others want to do better, they did the Christmas parties and company picnics, they gave awards, all the things others companies did. The problem was they did not have a plan, not a real plan for growth. They had a plan for getting more business. They were great salespeople, but a real plan would have also included growth.

They put too much in the hands of people who they thought would want to work hard for them because they were the highest paid and could take a good ass chewing. They believed in intimidation management. They would praise the good and rip ass on anyone they thought had anything to do with something that went wrong. They didn't have a development plan, they didn't have a training plan, and they didn't educate the people they wanted to be in charge. There was no person in charge of teaching employees the company's message and philosophies, mostly because they didn't have any.

The estimators brought the projects in, the operations department put crews on the jobs, and everyone involved with management would jump in and fix the problems long after they happened and soon after they found out about them. They learned after the complaints and after the unhappy customers' phone calls.

The plan was built around inexperienced people who were chosen because of their length of tenure or their abilities to be tough and intimidating, and were experts in ripping ass. My buddy who originally got me the job there moved on after a year or two, mainly because of these same reasons and because of an opportunity to go to another company. The company gave me the nod to take over.

I started with a thoughtful plan: Do nothing for at least one month and absorb what the company is doing right and what the company can do better. Then I went to the other superintendents and held several meetings about the changes I wanted to make and the changes they felt needed to be made. We collectively came up with our plan and message, began training programs, and put together project forms for daily reporting on the project. We also made great effort in finding the right foreman and crew for the right types of projects.

Some foremen were great at the larger projects, and some foremen were not ready to take on large projects but could learn in time. They could learn and be ready soon. Instead of yelling at them, we put them on smaller projects and spent more of our time with them instead of with the foremen who had more experience and needed less training. We had them run smaller projects and gave them larger projects as they grew.

You need to put together a plan, and it should not be a plan to do everything by yourself. You can't do it all by yourself.

With the owner's involvement, of course, and the help of the superintendents, we developed a plan to make the company bigger and better. With a well-thought-out plan, the company became quite large, and from the hard work of the many people who worked there, the owners happily sold the company several years later.

A plan can be many things. It can be about you making a life or career change, helping out with a charity or church, taking over a new position, or running a football team. It's time to get with yours.

4

Think About It First

Just like many kids, I also grew up a very troubled kid and a very poor kid. I had troubles many of the other kids couldn't even understand if I told them. Things like the electricity was turned off when I came home from school, or other times I would find the landlord sitting on our front porch looking for his overdue rent and asking me if I knew where my stepfather was, or being in fistfights, going blow to blows with my stepfather when I was at the very young age of thirteen, just completely unimaginable things like that they just could not imagine. Things I find troubling to think about even today.

My brother and I would save what little money we made by mowing lawns, painting fences, yard cleaning, you know things like that, only to have our stepfather find out about our little savings and then ask to borrow it (take it) with a shallow promise to pay it back. Which he never did! Most of the Pinole kids had what they needed and were raised in a normal household, they would not understand my problems nor would I want to speak of it to them.

I found football to be a big escape and a big help to me. I was good at it, and for just a few hours, I was the same as the other kids. No one was rich, and no one was poor. I was very fortunate to have the kind of coaches I had. They didn't give me any special treatment; they just didn't give me unnecessary grief. Russ Galvin reminded me of the coaches I had growing up, just good simple people. Russ also had a similar childhood as me, and together we used our troubled childhood experiences and the blessing we were given to coach football and used them to help a few kids get through a tough day or two. I really believe that good coaches have been given a blessing, they have an unusual need to help others and not just because they had a troubled childhood or had some horrible experience in their lives; that may have been the path Russ and I were given, but I believe good people and good coaches have been blessed with a large unselfish heart; they just get it. So here is a question I have trouble understanding: How could there be coaches who don't understand the blessings they have been given to do the right thing for these kids? I'm not talking about the dad who is helping coach because his son or daughter is playing, I'm talking about the youth and high school coaches who love the game and consider themselves as coaches, they are at practice and they work the sidelines year after year whether their kids are playing or not.

If you had a mean yelling guy for a coach when you played a sport and did not like or respect him for it, then why would you be a mean yelling coach when you get the chance to be a coach? Did you somehow like the coach who was ripping your butt more than the coach who was teaching you the sport? I am betting not! So why would you be like that coach? If you had a great coach and you liked him a lot, then why don't you coach like him? Really, you have to ask yourself, "Why am I being so mean to these kids? They just want to learn." I'm betting that most coaches who scream and yell do it because they cannot articulate their coaching points very well. It's not the player's inabilities or lack of desire to learn. Why don't coaches understand that they will get more from a kid by teaching and coaching than they will by screaming? Why don't they start to embrace the opportunity to do good for someone else by teaching? Slow things down for the players who are having trouble understanding your coaching points and teach them. Try a different approach if need be but keep teaching your points and they will get them eventually. Screaming at them will lock their mind down and you may never reach them that way. It's frustrating, I know, but remembering why you're there and the fun everyone can have should get you looking at it as a challenge, so embrace it and teach. It truly is a reward you have been given in coaching other people's children and having an opportunity in creating a fun and exciting season for everyone involved.

After several years of coaching with the varsity at Clayton Valley, I was ready for a new challenge, and one was presented. A friend of mine was asked to be the head coach at Concord High School. He was also an assistant coach with me at Clayton Valley. This coach and I discussed me working with him as assistant head coach and running backs coach. I was ready to make the move. This program prior to my friend taking over only won a few games in four seasons. Part of my role was to teach the offensive and defensive coordinators their positions more from a parent relations side than X's and O's. These coaches were very good assistants at Clayton, and they were years younger than me and not really ready for the challenges ahead of them. It did not take long before the egos took over and the frustrations in working with these young coaches took its toll on me. People around me were changing and the focus was no longer for the kids. Over a two-year stretch, I did all I could to make things right and get the program back in shape, and once it was obvious to me it wasn't going to happen, I decided to leave.

Understanding your reason for coaching will help you understand what you are trying to get out of it. If you feel fortunate to be coaching, then you will coach with an open mind, and if you coach with a thankful attitude, the players and the other coaches will adapt to the energy you have, and when you know you've been blessed to coach, you will finally have more joy in coaching and so will everyone around you, whether you're winning or losing.

I tried to work things out until I had enough. I held meetings, implemented policy changes, had the assistants meet one on one with the coordinators, but nothing was cracking those egos. Then it got worse. The assistants gave up and the communication went to hell, and I felt I would be better served to do something else, something that could help parents, players, and coaches (maybe write a book?).

The sad thing is these young coaches had the same beliefs about coaching as I did, but the pressure of winning got to them and they allowed their ethics and principles to change. These coaches, when at Clayton realized how fortunate they were in coaching, and they always had the kids, the parents, and the community first. By allowing themselves to fall under the pressures to win, they lost a little bit of the reasons they wanted to coach in the first place. They got what they wished for, they just weren't ready for all that came with it. The head coach and I had dinner the other night and he expressed to me how things changed after I left; he said the coaching staff and he are back with the focus of doing what is right for the kids, and things are going pretty well now at Concord High School. They made the playoffs, and the program has regained its support from the parents. What's really great is the kids and the parents and the coaches are back having fun.

As I mentioned before, coaching and business have a lot of similarities, and many people hunger to be the person in charge of them, but are they ready to do it right? Be careful what you wish for when you want to be the person in charge of a team or a business, because if you don't really understand what it's all about, you may find yourself in over your head, and if you are, even more reason to communicate with all your assistants. You may want to run your own business or be a construction superintendent, and that is all fine, and I applaud people who want to better themselves, but "Think About It First" and ask yourself these three questions: #1. Why are you doing this? #2. Will you make it better for others? #3. What could go wrong and will you have a plan for it?

If you think of these things first, you may realize (should you get the opportunity) that you will need to really understand what could be needed from you, and you should have a positive plan in place to handle what you think is coming as well as what you think could be coming, because you will be tested, and if your plan is based on personal satisfaction, you may find it difficult to stay on top. Stay with your good ethics and your good principles and use good character all the time; that would be the plan I would recommend for you.

There is nothing wrong in wanting to be a coach or business manager, but wishing to be one of these volunteers or business professionals without having a plan that will include needs of players, parents, other coaches, administrators, employees, coworkers, and clients is just being selfish, and you may find yourself wondering, Why did I wish for this job?

If you look around at work, you may see the one superintendent everyone likes to work with; you may hear an estimator in your office saying to the other estimators, "I sure hope I get Superintendent Jose on my job," or you may listen to one foreman bragging to the other foremen that he will be working with Superintendent Robbie on the project he was asked to run. Why do you think that is? Why do you think some superintendents are liked more than others? Because they have a plan, and they are confident in their plan, and they spread their confidence onto the people they are overseeing. They were careful in what they were planning to do and they knew what the entire job would require from them, good and bad, before they asked for it. Just like the title of a song from the Zac Brown Band, They got, "whatever it is," and that is tough to teach.

Once you lose touch with the fun and reward of being a business owner or a construction superintendent, you will start to self-destruct, and everything will become more of burden than a blessing.

These types of leaders don't want to listen to anyone who has advice or is willing to help them. They don't want to be told when they are not following the plan. No, they would rather blame others for their shortfalls and failures. When I speak to the superintendents or the project managers who work with me, I remind them often to understand the difficulties there are in managing others and to take responsibility for who they are and how they affect the people around them, because just like coaching football, work should be fun too.

I started working in the asbestos abatement industry back in 1986. I was working for a large insulation company that was just getting started in the abatement industry. They were about two years into it before I was employed there. The owner was a very sharp man and very driven by the dollar. He once said to me, "I want to be a millionaire before I'm thirty-three years old." I thought to myself, "What a tool." This guy was only going to be happy by making money.

Not such a bad thing, having goals to make money. We all need some, so why not? The point is this: If that is your only reason for being in business, I feel sorry for you.

You have issues if you choose to hold people down, if it makes you money. There are many stories about these types of leaders, some good and some bad. In most cases, these types of leaders will have early success and then find themselves in trouble because they are not capable of fixing problems that are caused by them. Yes, I said "caused by them." You see, they can tell you what you need to be doing and they are good at finding blame anywhere else they can find it, but when it comes to a conclusion that they may be the problem, with their policies or their lack of discipline or their greed, they just cannot see it. They don't have a plan to help others, and they don't share in the credit when things are going well; no, they just belittle those under them and they must pin the blame on someone else. Had they used their ethics and principles from the very beginning, and had they had a plan that included everyone, it would have created a better working environment for all.

I moved up pretty fast in that large abatement company, and after about six years of working there, I decided to go on my own. I got my general contractor's and hazardous abatement licenses and was doing some weekend work when the news came that the large abatement company was selling out to a computer firm and was no longer going to assist their clients. It seemed like bad news, except I had my license and was ready to take on the world.

Hang on. Not so fast. I was doing very little work and knew nothing about the accounting part of the business, so I was a little concerned. Luckily, that's when my colleagues and future partners Mike Christie, Rick Cleveland, and Marvin Henderson came to me and said, "We know you have your license and the operational background. We have the client relationships, and with Rick having his accounting degree, let's go get the business the other company was letting go."

I thought we could make this work. So the first thought I had was, "This is perfect. However, will it work?" These guys were very different from me in a lot of ways, some better, and some worse. I took some time and realized that even though we were all a little different from each other, we still cared about the same things. We still had the same principles. We were all good family people, and I was sure their character would get better from being around me. (I'm joking, of course.) "Let's do it," I said. This has been going on since 1993, and I'm very proud of all of us.

We have two companies now: Bayview Environmental Services (1993) and Demo Masters (2001). My background in business is more on the operational side of things, and this is why I can see the similarities in coaching and business. Operations in a construction company run just like a football program. You still need to surround yourself with good hard working people and you have to have the right players in the right spots. Every man or woman has a place and position to play. You cannot have a partner or coach sending a different message than yours. All leaders must first agree on the message for the program or business plan, and then it must not change unless all partners change it together, and never in front of a player or employee. You cannot build something when the people around you have different principles or if they have a selfish character looking for ways to make the plan work out solely for their own benefit.

It's critical in any business plan to use and stay with your ethics and principles all the time, even when it may not seem popular. Some of my day-to-day duties at Demo Masters are overseeing the operations and estimating for the company, and along with that, I am responsible for the revenue the company brings in. We had been working with a general contracting company for some time, and they were not really much of a source of revenue for us. I started to market them more, not being very careful of who I was looking to work with, and soon they started giving Demo Masters some pretty good-sized projects. We would perform the work without complaints, but weeks later, we would receive a call about a back charge they were imposing on us, back charges we knew nothing about and back charges they had no paperwork for.

This happened on every single project we did with them. It came to my attention that every time we did a job with these guys, Demo Masters would end up losing money. We just could not make our profit margins with this company. I went back and pulled up all of the projects we ran over the last year and found three projects that did not make money. Yes, it was this same company. The only three projects that lost money were the three projects we did with them.

Now, if I had pulled the reports and had five projects that lost money and it was a mix of different contractors, then that would be on Demo Masters and I would need to change some things up in-house. However, if it is three projects and all three are with the same company, there may be a pattern here. This company would bill us for deductive change orders that we knew nothing about, would back charge us for damage we knew nothing about, held our payments more than 120 days, and so on. I needed to make a call, and I did. I explained to them that our business plan no longer included them, and we would not do business with them anymore. I also explained that it wasn't personal, sometimes companies are just not compatible. Their business plan included cheating people out of something to have personal gain. Simply put, they were just not like my partners and me. Everyone in business is in business to make some profit, you don't need to be so greedy that your plan is to make your profit by making other companies lose theirs, that is just nuts.

Six years later, we ran into another company, this one based out of San Francisco. Again not being careful, we marketed them hard, and soon they too asked us to work on some of their projects. Things went pretty well with this company for several years. Then they started their own demolition company, without telling anyone. Once we confronted them for doing their own demolition, they said it was small and they only did minor work. We were fine with that until the following year, when they asked

Demo Masters to bid their projects against two other demolition contractors and them. After they received bids from everyone, they told us they looked over the bids and their own numbers were lower than ours.

"No kidding," I said. "Next time maybe you could let me open the bids."

Anyway, in their defense, they claimed to have a system that was fair, but I never saw it that way. I just knew that they were not the kind of people that I needed to be working with, and it certainly was not the type of company we were looking for to work with.

I gave them the same speech about the two companies business plans just not being compatible, and we both moved on.

There are too many really great companies out there looking to do the right thing, and we are that way. So why settle for some company that's not working with the same principles you are? I guarantee you that the longtime running and standing companies did not get there because they cheated everyone along the way. Don't forget, all the subcontractors talk to each other. They know who was cheated and by whom. After a period of time, those types of general contractors get higher bids by all the subcontractors (if they get any at all) and start to find they are no longer competitive.

So we very politely explained to them it was time for us to make a change. I don't have a problem with them wanting to do their own demolition. That's a business choice, and good for them to keep people working. I just don't think that their demolition subcontractors are as happy for them as they think.

You would not ask a waiter to get you a window seat at a really nice restaurant and then open up your bag of McDonald's and eat it there, would you? Use your head. Not everyone is a dummy. When you start to think that some other business owner is so stupid that he or she would give you pricing for the same work that you do because you said you had a fair program, is insulting. Then again, maybe there is one dummy in the room.

I'm not saying never wish for success or never wish for something challenging. I'm just saying "Think About It First."

5

Let Them Be Proud Too

I find it a little crazy when I see youth football coaches getting in the faces of young players, then screaming and yelling at them as if they are not trying to do well or as if they are not trying to understand whatever the lesson is that these short-tempered coaches are trying to teach. You see, I believe these coaches are having trouble expressing their teaching points to the players. These coaches are getting frustrated because they cannot be understood. The coach needs to step back and realize these players don't want to disappoint them. They want to be successful and make their coach proud. They want to go home and tell their parents about how well they did at practice that day and make Mom and Dad proud of them too.

The coach needs to work on a better way to get his points understood. He should evaluate the level of his player's skill and put those thoughts into his plan when teaching a technique or fundamental drill. Some players will pick up on a drill faster than others. Some may be physically able to do the drill but mentally will forget an angle move or be a slow thinker on the coverage part of a drill, even if the coach just explained it. Some players will mentally understand the coach's concept of the drill and be quick thinkers only to physically trip over their own feet. Getting in their face and ripping all over them won't fix this problem nor will it instill confidence in them.

No, the coach needs to evaluate all players and determine which ones will need more one-on-one time. The coach should keep his position drills set up for all his players, not singling anyone out. As players develop in the group, the coach should be sure to praise the ones doing well in the drills and use them as examples for the other kids to get a visual lesson. Then they should pull aside the ones who need a little more instruction and give them extra time. This works best if you have an assistant coach with you, because the assistant can run your drills with the group while you spend time instructing an individual who needs some one-on-one time. This hopefully is the reason you wanted to be a coach in the first place.

You should want to teach and be right there in the action to give some of that one-on-one time to these players and watch them get better as football players. Look into their faces to see their wondering eyes looking for ways to get better, and after a couple of weeks of your one-on-one instructions, look into those same faces, and you'll see those eyes now filled with confidence and determination because these players have improved and know it. And you'll feel great too, because you took the time to reach and teach the players. You didn't break down any players by screaming at them. You just realized that everyone is a little different, and they needed some coaching.

Anyone can coach a great athlete, but a great coach will help an athlete be great. You take a player with a little bit of talent and develop the player into one who becomes very good and is having a great time with the sport, and you start to see them succeed in this sport. You tell your friends and family about how proud you are of what you have done with this player, and you are very proud of the player who worked so hard. So let them be proud too.

You don't have to scream and yell at players to get them to perform. They all want to perform. These kids are not going out for football so they don't have to go home after school and mow the lawn. They want to be football players. It's just that some are not as good as they may think, and when you yell at them, all you're doing is demeaning them. They will lose confidence and won't have a lot of respect for you as a coach.

Coaches are usually ex-players, and we can be a little cocky too. And when we coach a kid up, we are pretty proud of ourselves. Well, they have a right to be proud too. They also are working very hard, and they should not have to be taught by some screaming coach who never had a plan or was not prepared to teach players the game. They like to go home and speak to their families the same as the coach does and express the feelings of the pride they have in themselves and the game.

A coach who can't communicate with all players and gets himself frustrated and starts screaming at the players is a coach who I believe will never reach his own goals. And I'll bet you he blames the players every time something goes wrong. This is the type of coach who, after a game is over and they lost the game, would say something like, "The kids just got outplayed today," or "Our kids just made too many mistakes." They will never take any of the blame. It's always the kids. However, in the rarity that they win a game, they say, "Boy, that was brilliant coaching today. I had a great game plan," or "I told you kids this week at practice, 'If you don't make mistakes, I will find a way to win.'" What a treat to have this horn-blower for a coach. What a joke. Unfortunately, they are out there. Believe me. I have seen them up close, and I have even worked with a few.

Most of you can see it coming because people don't change much. You can see it in the way they live as adults. Look at it this way. If you meet your kid's youth football coach on the first day and his car is a total mess, his shirt needs stain remover, and he has his paperwork in a wadded-up super-old folder with his favorite professional football team sticker on it, I'm betting he's unorganized and not big on teaching kids to be proud.

Now, if you meet your kid's youth football coach on the first day and he has a detailed, clean work truck, and he is wearing a clean shirt that fits, and his paperwork is neatly stored in a file box with alphabetical labels, I'm betting he's organized and a little bit controlling but will seek pride in all around him.

You see, most coaches in youth and high school football levels are ex-players, P.E. teachers, dads, and volunteers. They all have other real-life jobs. Some may not be very high up in their companies, they may be underappreciated at work, they may be going through hard times, and they may become high-strung and ultimately are looking to vent off some work-related stress. They have some football experience and want to coach so they can be in charge of something. They try to intimidate the players and parents and they act like they are bigger than the program itself. They have no pride. These are the coaches you need to keep an eye on because they can be dangerous and hurtful to these young players.

A coach who wants to teach players with passion and technique and fundamentals is the kind of coach you want your kids around. These types of coaches will work well with all players of all levels. These coaches will take pride in the improvement of all players and understand what it means to have a successful season even if they didn't get all the wins they wanted but find the year a success because of the players' improvement. And at the end of the year, everyone goes home proud of themselves. Believe me. They are out there too.

I don't think coaches, managers, principals, superintendents, or any other people who are in charge of players, coworkers, assistant coaches, or their subordinates understand how important it is to downplay your authority a little bit. I think you will get people working harder for you if you are not constantly reminding them that they work for you, not with you. You can't go around and joke with them by saying things like, "Don't forget. I can fire you," or saying things like, "Well, I'm your boss, so we are going to do it my way." You are just being negative, and your staff will never gain confidence or feel secure, besides the fact they will think you're an ass for acting that way and will never give you any respect. I'm sure it has something to do with your own ego or insecurities, but I'm not an expert on that. It's best to manage the business at hand.

If you're coaching a team or running a business and you are the main person in charge, you want to manage those plans and the messages that have been built. You don't need to remind everyone that you're in charge, especially if you are the guy who won't take any of the blame when it all goes wrong. What I mean here is the business or the football team has a plan and the message in place because you and your coworkers or assistant coaches set one up already. You and they together put the plan in place. Everyone knows that you're the president or the head coach, and of course you have final say. After all, when it does go downhill, you're the one getting blamed or fired. However, downplay your role as leader by getting people to buy in on working together as a unit. Convince them that everyone is working together as equals. No one has more say than the other. Coaches or managers will discuss issues together, and there will be a vote on all major issues. However, nobody changes the plan and message without all leaders' knowledge and involvement. Now everyone is working together, and the core of the plan and message is intact, and no one feels threatened or insecure. They all believe in the system because they are a part of building it. They will take ownership of it, and they will be proud of it, as you are.

Our company plan at Demo Masters is just like the one at Bayview Environmental. My partners and I built the Bayview plan, and it worked so well we used the same model when we started Demo Masters. Our plan is to provide quality service and fair pricing to our customers. We believe our work is so good, in some cases we offer a 100 percent satisfaction guarantee or we do the work for cost. We have a positive marketing plan that all employees participate in. We create opportunities for our employees and are an equal opportunity employer. And as the principals of these companies, we are proud to be an employee-owned company, and the employees are proud to be a part of it as well.

I spend most of my time running Demo Masters, and I do it with an open-door policy. It's open to all employees, from the person sweeping floors to the general superintendent. I have this policy in place to keep order in the company plan. The company's plan has to remain intact at all times. The company's plan is larger than any employee, and it's larger than me. We built our company's plan to run on its own. If your plan is built right, it will survive even if you or several other important people leave because it's built to run with everyone's involvement. It can't weaken, because it's built for the next person to take over should someone need or want to move on.

If you as the leader in charge of the plan commit to it and don't put yourself above it, then it will get bigger and stronger with time. If built right, you have the top leaders working with and teaching the people below them, and they in return work with and teach the people below them, and so on. Everyone has involvement, and there is some form of double coverage in all areas for your business. These concepts will work with your football team also if the head coach works with the assistant head coach, and the assistant head coach works with the coordinators, and the coordinators work with the coaches, and so on. Teaching and learning each other's duties will give your system strength and consistency. When you build something that is this strong, and you are motivating coworkers or teammates, and the company or team is a winner, everyone is proud to be a part of it, and they will not allow it to fail. It starts with you at the top, sticking to the plan and allowing it to grow and downplaying your role as the leader to allow others to take part in the system.

I meet once a week with our superintendents after our operations meetings on Thursdays. We review our job board for projects that are ongoing and are up-and-coming. We discuss the teachings of the foremen below the superintendents. We discuss the company plan and message every week. I spend a lot of time with these superintendents because it is very important that they hear from me weekly about my commitment to the plan. I cannot allow these guys to forget what we are trying to build and give to our clients. If they see that I am not committed, then they will become less interested in it. However, if they see me committed to it and they hear me comment on it on a regular basis, they teach the people below them. And when they see that I'm not insecure about my position and others learning what I do, they won't be either.

The same thing works with your football team. Teach your coaches what you know, and show them how committed you are to the plan. Have them teach the coaches below them, and keep the message alive. It will amaze you how everyone around you will start taking pride in what they are doing when you have a winning plan.

I have also had many conversations with my superintendents about how they work with the people who are below them. Not everyone is instantly ready to be taught. Some have a hard time with it, but it is normal because they are very proud people and need to be appreciated and may feel like you're doing this to downgrade them. They may even be a little insecure.

I am not the yelling type, and I don't believe any leader needs to be. That type of behavior is not in our plan. Our plan is about teaching and convincing our employees to get better and grow to service our clients with pride.

I remind our superintendents that they have foremen who look up to them and are eager to learn from them. And if they handle this correctly, these foremen will pass on their knowledge to the leadmen who follow them. I often tell them some true stories that I have experienced over the years when I was a superintendent at another construction company prior to starting my own.

One that comes to mind is about a night job we had. It started at 6:00 PM and went until 2:30 AM MONDAY THROUGH FRIDAY. The project was at one of the Embarcadero Buildings in San Francisco. I had a foreman working on the project, and it was nearing the end, and I was getting concerned that we were not going to make the deadline, which was the following Friday. I would show up a couple of nights a week to see how he was doing, and one night it appeared to me that the foreman's crew was scattered all over the floor. I saw guys on both ends of the floor cleaning up debris and moving it to different sides of the building, then hauling it out of one side of the building. This was not typical of how we did things.

The project looked like it had a lot of work to get finished by the deadline, and I thought it needed a better plan. I discussed with my foreman that I wanted to bring everyone to the same side of the floor to work together, moving in one direction. I also reminded him that this coming Friday was the deadline, and it had to get done by then. He agreed that Friday was doable; however, he wanted to continue with the plan he had. He said his plan was better because every evening around midnight, the janitors gave up the elevator that they used for removing building trash, and this allowed us to off-load from both sides of the floor. He also said he would be able to complete the project by Friday if I allowed him to do it his way.

I gave this some thought, and I said, "Okay. Let's do it your way." And to his credit, he pulled it off. We completed the project on time, and his plan worked to perfection. About three weeks later, I ran into this foreman again at the office, and I told him once more that he did a great job on that project. He told me something I'll never forget. He said, "That next morning after I had asked you if I could finish the project with my plan and you said yes, I told my wife that there was no way I'd let it fail. This was my idea, and I needed to make it work. And I have never been so proud that I did it."

The lesson here for my superintendents is that it was my responsibility to get the project done by that Friday, and it didn't matter if it was going to get done with my ideas or his. But if he has an idea that will work, let him have it. He will take ownership of it, and he and his family will be proud of what he and everyone accomplished.

The superintendents and I meet every week formally, but we talk every day. The plan is that important. Talking about it, believing in it, and staying consistent with it, so everyone knows the importance of it and should be a part of the plan.

The open-door policy I have is there to keep everyone focused on the plan. It allows me to remind people that their position is one to be proud of, but if you are not using it properly, the plan will go into action. Here is an example of how the plan will take over: Let's say a laborer is working on a project with a foreman, and the laborer feels he is being mistreated by this foreman, and he wants to speak to me about it. He can. I have the door wide open, and I want to hear what this laborer has to say because my partners and I want every employee to have a chance to succeed. We have a plan in place for this.

I will call the foreman in along with his superintendent, and we will discuss the problem that this laborer is reporting. We discuss it in detail, and then I will handle it as needed. I will explain the plan and our message again to this foreman. If the foreman is in the wrong, then he will be reprimanded, and the laborer will move to another project. If the laborer is in the wrong, I will explain the plan to him and why I want the foreman doing things he finds troubling. He will be returned to the same project or moved to another one if he chooses.

Now, whether the foreman was right or wrong here doesn't matter. What matters here is everyone has a shot at being heard. This also helps keep cliques and groups from forming, which is something else I don't believe in. There should only be one clique or group, and that is our united plan.

6

It's Their Time

You may still remember many good times from your youth and high school football-playing days. I started playing when I was twelve years old for the Pinole Junior Spartans football team. The Pop Warner football teams back then only had players twelve to fourteen years old. After that, it was on to high school football. There were no Junior Pee Wee, Pee Wee, Junior Midget, and Midget teams like there are now. We just had the one. I would have loved to have played sooner if the younger programs were around back then. I just could not get enough football. I remember my first tryouts. I was a pretty fast runner, a tough kid, and very small for my age, but I didn't give it much thought because I knew I could play.

The Youth Football League had rules similar to the ones now, that every kid must have completed ten hours of conditioning before they could wear the issued uniforms, you know, the shoulder pads, helmet, chin strap, girdle filled with hip pads, practice jersey, pants with the thigh pads, knee pads, of course the really large cup that you had to ask a returning player how to put on, and the mouthpiece that you had to boil at home in hot water to form to your teeth.

I remember how awesome it was when we completed our last day of conditioning. We all went to the head coach's house, where he had his garage door opened, and we got in line with the other players and waited to pick out our stuff. I remember my shoulder pads were so big they would flap up and down on me when I ran. These days, football players have their equipment fitted, but back then, no one was really checking. I didn't care what kind of pads I had. I just wanted to play football.

I remember one practice where we were all in a drill called "Bull in the Ring." This is where all the players form a large circle and then hold hands and create a link. There is one player who starts in the middle of the circle, and the coach will point at random at a player who is part of the circle and blow his whistle. Once the whistle is blown, the person who was pointed out charges the player in the middle for what would hopefully be a big collision.

It was my first time in this drill, and after a couple of players went through the hitting machine, I was called out as the random player and was going up against the largest, toughest player we ever had. This guy in the middle of the ring was kicking everyone's butt, and no one wanted to go up against him. I was not the exception. The whistle blew, and I ran out there. Needless to say, I got racked so hard I fell to my knees. Everyone busted out laughing. I looked up and started laughing too. I got up and said, "Let's go again," and we did. This time he drilled me into the ground, and I pulled my face from the turf. I said, "Let's go again." This went on about three or four times, and the coach said to me, with laughter in his voice, "Okay, Mini-Stud. That's enough." And throughout my couple of years there in Pop Warner football, that was my nickname: Mini-Stud. (This drill is outlawed now because it causes a lot of injuries. Please don't ever use it.)

For my last year in Pop Warner football, my coaches wanted me to be the quarterback. I said, "No way. I want to be the running back and play defense, and you coaches don't let your quarterback play defense. I also want to play linebacker." I was one of the best players on this team, and I did not want to sit and watch when my teammates were out there on defense. This was my time to play, and I wanted to play a lot, and besides the fact, it was not a good football coaching decision. We had another kid who was pretty good at quarterback who didn't want to play defense. He just wanted to be a quarterback. I was a good running back and also good on the defensive side of the ball. The coaches finally agreed to the no-brainer argument I was trying to make, and we moved on.

We completed our conditioning week and headed over to the head coach's house to pick up our pads. I noticed that the head coach had set all of my equipment aside, and there was a small set, quarterback size, of shoulder pads there too. I asked the coach why.

He said, "Donnie, I need you to play quarterback for us this year. You are the best we got."

I said, "No way. I told you this was my last year, and I want to break some of the running back records, and I want to play defense. Come on. This is my time."

He said, "If you don't play quarterback, then you don't play at all."

I looked at my stepdad, and I said sadly, "Let's go home." I walked down the coach's driveway and got in the car.

Coach ran down the driveway, looked at me in the window, and said, "Okay, kid. You win."

What is so wrong with letting the kids play where they want to play? Quarterback, running back, tight end, who cares? It is their time. You can try to put players where they have a better chance to succeed, but I think you have to do that after they try out in the position that they dream to play.

I had a kid who I thought would be great at fullback for us, and I asked him if he would like to play that position. He said to me, "Not really, Coach Howell. I want to play quarterback."

I said, "Okay. Then let's get you over there with the quarterbacks so you can compete for playing time."

I gave it a couple of days because I knew he would not make it over there. We had some really good returning quarterbacks. I was hoping for him, but I knew it wouldn't work, and I understood he had to learn it for himself. After a few days, I asked him how it was going over there for him. He said, "Not so good," but he was interested in fullback if I still wanted him. I told him I was so excited that he was coming over, and I was saving the position just in case he wanted it.

He played very well at fullback and was a successful player for us. I'm sure he will tell his stories someday of the fun he had during his time in high school football. He might not have worked that hard at being a fullback if in the back of his mind he thought I was cheating him out of being a quarterback for my own benefit. Let the kids try to accomplish their goals before you step in. This is their time to enjoy the game. You enjoyed yours, didn't you?

High school was just as much fun as youth football, as I remember. A lot of the kids were the ones I played with in youth football, and over the summer, we all got a little bigger.

We had some really good coaches at Pinole Valley High School. Our coaches were known for their football knowledge and the toughness they instilled in their players. They were great people to be around too. They made sure the players on their teams were held accountable for any trouble they caused, on or off the field. They also understood that it was our time to enjoy the game and all that went with it. They also understood that this was high school football, and most kids would never put on football pads again after high school was over. They understood that very few players go on to play college football, or even junior college football, for that matter. They understood very well this would be the end of the road for many of these kids, so why not let them enjoy what was left?

These coaches would never let a second- or third-string player sit on the bench in a game where we were leading 20 to 0 with three minutes left just so they could save a shutout. These coaches would never tell a player that they could not try out for a position that they may have wanted to play. "Give it your best shot," is what they would say to the player. These coaches would do whatever they could do to get us ready to win a game. They would do it in a way that everyone supported because whether you were the first-string, second-string, or third-string, you played at least a little. These coaches didn't have players showing up at practice holding blocking bags and shields all week just to become a sideline spectator at the Friday night games.

These coaches didn't want any of their second- and third-string players going into a game unprepared either. They got some reps in practice, and when they did get their reps, us first-stringers held the bags. We were no better than the players who held the bags for us. Everyone who was holding a bag was helping coach the other players. So everyone was coached up at practice, and everyone got in some reps as well. Sure, the number ones got a little more rep time, but that's needed for timing reasons, and we earned it.

These coaches had something going on that was special. They were unselfish coaches who were winners and who understood that it was our turn to enjoy high school football. They never for one second thought their job was to be the cool guy with the parents and fans. Nope. They just wanted to build football players and a winning organization. They wanted us to enjoy our time. As coaches, they knew that most kids were not going any further in this sport after high school. They simply didn't have the talent. But they also didn't see any reason to make you regret playing football and enjoying the time you had either.

I wish more coaches would think and act like these coaches, because they really understood this stuff, and in return, they got rewarded for it. They got more rewards from more players and parents than most of the egotistical coaches are trying to get.

I still see many of my high school teammates, and I still see and play golf with my former coaches. I do this because I want to. I want to be around my former coaches because they have great principles and ethics, and they are winners.

We won the North Coast Championship my senior year, and these coaches and my underclassmates won it again the next year. These coaches also won a couple of Turkey Bowls before the North Coast Section Playoffs were developed. These coaches understood that you could win without tearing someone else's high school football dreams apart.

Coaches are people who become a part of your life's story. They are not the life story. A coach needs to understand that kids come from all walks of life. Some have great parents, and some do not. Some have money, and some do not. Some need help with their schoolwork. Some are bothered by some kind of personal problem. But they are all young people who need a coach to teach them this sport, and they need a mentor to be there when they ask. They need you to ask them about their day once in a while.

What they really don't need is a coach who will go out of his or her way to become another problem for them. They don't need a coach who really was not very good in high school or never played college, who goes around telling people that he or she did play somewhere that is just not true, and wants to bully or take it out on these players. It's their time now.

I was driving my truck one day to check up on a project we had at the Presidio Naval Hospital in San Francisco, and I saw a picture of a homeless man taped to a street sign. Under the photograph of this person someone wrote, "Stephen, we love you."

And I thought to myself, "Everybody has as a mom or a dad who loves him or her, no matter what he or she did or what he or she has become. This was someone's child, and they cared about him enough to place a sign on a street post." I don't know if he was missing or presumed dead. I just know he had a mom and dad somewhere who cared about him.

Every player you have as a coach is someone's child, and they are loved very much by him or her. You are spending time with someone's child, and you should think of that as an honor and realize that it doesn't matter if you like the kid personally or not. You are there to make them all better football players, and some will be better than others. Some of these kids will still turn out to be great adults, great parents someday, or even good coaches later in life, even if they are not great at throwing a ball or catching a pass. These young people have family members who care about them very much, just like you do with yours. You would be extremely upset if you knew that a coach was mistreating your kid. The coach is supposed to be teaching him or her the sport, and if you found out they were treating your kid unfairly instead, it would get you pissed off.

I hope you will become a coach who gets it and understands, like my coaches did. I know I learned a lot from them, and I never coached any other way. When I go to the grocery store here in town, I often run into former players of mine, who say, "Hello, Coach Howell," and I get a hug. And I see former players' parents, and they stop and ask if I will ever come back and coach. They miss having me around, and I could not be prouder of that.

When it comes to business, I still maintain these thoughts of treating people who work for me fairly. I think sometimes you need to change things up a little to get it fair for everyone.

One of the things I changed once I started running Demo Masters was something that I believed was built into the system that was unfair to some of the employees. Not intentionally, of course. It was a small company when we started it, and we had three or four very, very good foremen and an excellent superintendent. We did move it up to seven or eight foremen but the problem was growing the company big. We had trouble getting bigger because some of the cliques we had needed to be separated. The company was also set up to where we only promoted people according to seniority. However, we could not grow because of this loyalty plan to the first foreman, then the second foreman, then the third foreman, and so on, in this order of promotions. One person could not jump another with less seniority. We also had a system where our foreman would work with his own crew, and these crewmembers always went with the same foreman to a project. This was the pecking order and system we had. It was not a bad one, really, it just wasn't designed for growth, in my opinion, and I was going to change it. But I had to be careful because of the pride that these employees had in our company, and they were a very big part of what we did. They were so dedicated that they really believed that this was their company, and it was their time to shine with it. But the system needed some change.

The problem we had was that when we were in need of another superintendent or general foreman, we would have to wait until foreman number one was ready to move up. If he wasn't ready, we just waited until he was ready or the need got so big we had to hire from outside. Not a bad plan for a smaller company.

In fact, it's a great plan for a smaller company. It shows loyalty to the employees, and you can set a pay scale based on seniority. However, I felt that there were some people who could move up immediately, and a change in business as usual would be good, and it might be someone else's time too.

We were able to wait out the changes for a little longer because Demo Masters merged with another successful demolition company based out of San Francisco. The company doubled the size of its labor force practically overnight. After several months of working through the merger, we looked at some changes. Along with our daytime superintendent, we needed a nighttime superintendent and a superintendent to work a split shift between the other superintendents (11:00 AM to 7:30 PM). This would blend the day work organization with the night work organization.

We did this by promoting foremen who were ready to move up, not by who had the most seniority. We also took into consideration someone's family life. If they had young kids, they should be and wanted to be at home at night, and other reasons like this. The foremen all knew who would be ready, and they also knew the other foremen who got passed up were still really good foremen but were lacking a little in English or had family issues or simple things like this. Nobody thinks any less of these foremen nor do they have any doubts of how important they are to this company, I just didn't want to put someone in a potions to fail.

We also changed the foreman-to-crew ratio. Instead of the foreman and the same crew on every project, we went to the foreman and his three best guys, and they would get three other guys to help teach each other different (and maybe better) ways to complete their work.

We also found out that we had plenty of laborers who were ready to become foremen. Some of these people were getting lost in the foremen-with-the-same-crew policy. The plan we have in place now will allow anyone to help grow and move within the company in the right direction, and it won't matter if there is someone who has been there longer than them. If you have been with Demo Masters and Bayview Environmental for a long time, then you are being looked at first of course.

People at Demo Masters and Bayview Environmental are being rewarded by the service they provide to our customers, their coworkers, and the company. Even in business, you can understand where people are, and you can care about where they want to go, and you can make changes that help some people without hurting others. Put some thought and care into it, and it can work out.

We understand, just like my coaches did, that our company is also their company. We need to make it a place that they want to come to. It needs to be a workplace that is comfortable, and it needs to be a place where everyone has a chance to grow. These people spend most of their day at work, and they should feel they have some say in what they can do for the company. We have some young people working in our office now who will someday take things over from us. I just hope we understand that it's their time to run things when the time comes.

7

Stand Up and Be Heard

That's your kid out there looking to have a good time playing football and wanting to have fun with his friends. He or she should not have to experience a coach who would take that away from them. You owe it to your child, yourself, and everyone else who has a kid who plays on the team to stand up and be heard. I don't want to sound like all youth football coaches are not very good. That would be an incorrect statement on my part. Actually, there are more good ones than bad ones, and in some cases, there are very good ones out there. I want you to be able to see the difference between the two early on; this way, you will be prepared to help correct the situation before you and your child have an unpleasant year.

Here is a little something for the moms and dads: In youth football, most coaches are dads, plain and simple. Sometimes, they become coaches because they have a kid who really is not a good football player at all but will be your team's starting quarterback if his dad is the coach, even if your kid is better and wants to play quarterback.

Some of these coaches just had the time that you didn't have to coach. It may be that they get off work at an earlier time, they work outside of the office, or maybe they work from home and schedule their own hours. It's not important why. They just have the time to take it all on. So this other dad takes the head coaching job that you couldn't, and his son gets to pick the position he wants to play first. This comes as no surprise to you because maybe your kid also played Little League baseball, and it's the same kind of thing in that sport too.

There are many reasons why people coach sports, and the point I'm trying to make here is that they need to do it for the right reasons. They should want to coach so they can spend more time with their child, and they should look at yours as if he or she was one of their own. They should take the game seriously and prepare kids to be ready for the next level of play. They need to come prepared with some football knowledge, a practice schedule, a plan for selecting assistant coaches, a game plan to motivate players, and hopefully a plan to win some football games. They need to be up front about how long they will stay coaching at that level of play. Are they leaving when their child moves up in the league, or are they there to coach for a long time? This information is needed so the parents who are working on the league board of directors can plan and start looking for a replacement. Either way is fine. They just need to be up front.

The problem I have with some of the coaches who play their kids over other people's kids, when the other kids are better, besides it being a bad principle, is that the other kids know who really is the better player, and the coach's kid also knows who is really the better player. This coach who thinks he is helping his kid really is hurting him more than helping him. The other kids will not be forgiving when they keep losing games because the coach's kid is not getting the job done. They won't want to be his friend either. Isn't that part of why you wanted your kids to play sports in the first place, so they could make friends and enjoy the game? These coaches put a lot of undue pressure on their own kids.

In most cases, you will just let it all happen. You won't say anything because you don't want your kid, your perfection, to get punished or put into the doghouse by some arrogant coach because you spoke up. These types of coaches may not even realize how much control they have on you, yet they know they have some.

Sometimes, you have to look at things from a different perspective. Let's go back to why some of these not-so-good coaches coach in the first place:

#1. Their kid is not that good and could get cut from the team. #2. The coach was never any good when he was in high school and wants to try again through his or her kid. #3. Nobody will have lunch with this coach at work, and the coach has no friends, so the coach thought, "Why not be in charge of something and control your kids?" (Okay, that's a stretch.)

Why would you just let this kind of coach control you and your family? Stand up and be heard. Most of the time, these types of coaches are not geared toward picking on just your kid. They are doing it to many, and I'll tell you why. They can't coach. They don't have a plan. They are not there for the right reasons. They have to look for great players to cover up their inabilities to coach. They are coaching at the youth level. Are you getting it? They are amateurs. They are regular people just like you. They don't have the credentials to run your life. You need to question them. You need to ask them for reasons that you can understand for what they are doing. You need to let them know that they have people to answer to as well.

If you have a coach who is working with your kids in a fashion that is unacceptable, you need to first talk to the coach. If you don't get anywhere with Mr. Neat Guy, go to some of the assistant coaches and express your feelings. If that is not working, go to the other parents, get a petition signed by the other parents, and take it to the board.

I'm not saying that youth or high school football coaches are all a bunch of tools, I'm just saying if you run across a bad coach, you should stop him or her from continuing to coach in a wrongful manner. You want your child to have a good time and learn about the game. If you don't speak up and you just let it go, these coaches will just become someone else's problem. They need to be removed from the system. Better yet, let's help them!

So if you can't spare the time to be the head coach or you don't know enough about the game to be an assistant coach, then why not offer to help on the days you can be there? Sometimes, helping with dressing the field or removing practice bags from the shed is a big help. There are a lot of little things you can do. Just ask the coach before practice starts on the days you are there. If you do know the sport and would like to help out, talk to the coach about being an assistant coach. If you have some high school experience or college, let the coach know. If you're a student of the game (whether you played or not) and would like to get into coaching, youth is a great place to start. If you are good at organizing things, see the coach. You may be helpful. Or maybe you would like to be the team mom or a team mom's helper. Get involved. The more you take a stake in the team, the more you will become closer to the people running it, and you will be able to spread your proper ethics and good principles around.

I don't believe anyone who wants to coach kids is trying to be a bad person or deliberately trying to treat people badly, but they do need to know when they are abusive, and they need to know they don't have the right to ruin the season that everyone else wants to have.

Starting from the first day when you meet your coach at the introductions meeting, ask your new coach to give you his plan for the kids. What are his coaching ethics, and what are his goals for the year? How will he pick his assistant coaches? What are his football practices like? Can you help in any way? If you're not sure what to ask, then review the Parent Cheat Sheet I've provided in back of this book.

Monitor what he says, and keep them on track throughout the year. You can politely remind a coach from time to time about the plan he gave you back on the first day you met.

If the coach really becomes a bad influence around your child or someone else's, talk to him about it. Talk to the assistant coaches about it. Talk to other parents about it. And if needed, get a petition signed by as many parents as you can, and get it to the board.

If we are talking about high school football here, then you can also go to the athletic director or the school principal and let them know who you have spoken to about the problem. Ask them to watch the coach at a practice, during a game, or wherever your issues are coming from, and let them see for themselves what is going on and ask them to give you their feedback. Football as well as any other sport should be a fun time for your child, yourself, and the coach. Get involved, and help steer it in the right direction.

My business partners and I meet every week, and we discuss the business financials, operations, future development of the companies, investments, and we even discuss and review our employees. The thing that is most impressive to me about those meetings is that we discuss everything in detail. We don't hurry through the meeting, nor do we rush someone who may be speaking in the meeting. In our meetings, the floor is yours until you relinquish it, and nobody will stop you. When you're done, we vote.

Now, I may have had an idea or a comment on something, and when it was my turn, I would take the floor and express my views for as long as needed. And when I finished and gave up the floor, we would have a vote, and I could be outvoted. Then I would go with the vote. And as arrogant as I can be, I'm not so arrogant as to think I'm smarter individually than the other three partners are collectively, and they have the same understanding.

You speak your peace, and you go 100 percent with the majority decision. You sell the plan after the vote has been taken, whether it went your way or not. Everyone in our meetings has a right to stand up and be heard. It's a reasonable business plan, and as an individual, it's just being a mature person with a plan to make things work for everyone. It's being fair and respectful to everyone who is trying to move the plan in the same direction.

Whether you're in coaching or in business, take some time to hear the facts, and make the right call for everyone who is working hard to make things better for the plan, even if the idea or comment is not your own, but the suggestion will be best for the plan.

Then you need to make the change. Don't forget. You want the plan to be successful too, and if you let people around you have a chance to stand up and be heard and they actually see you making good decisions and making some sacrifices, then you will be as successful as the plan will be.

I have mentioned before that I have an open-door policy, and that is for the same reason as well. I want employees to be able to walk into my office any time, stand up, and be heard. If they feel I am sincere about it, and I am, then they will be comfortable saying anything to me about how to better run our business, they will take ownership in it, they will look out for it, and they will want to tell me about who isn't looking out for it. You can think you're the greatest businessperson out there, and you may be. But you will be a failure in business soon enough if your employees don't feel that they are a big part of the plan and if they feel they are constantly being told what to do. They won't care about anything but a paycheck. They already know that they are a big part of the business. So if you do everything yourself and you don't have any employees, then go ahead and pat yourself on the back. However, if you are like my partners and me, and you rely heavily on your employees, make sure you let them know. Be open with them.

Just because you have an open-door policy doesn't mean they have a good idea either. Never discourage them from standing up and being heard. Take the time to explain why their idea doesn't work so they can stay interested in helping and guiding the business in the right direction. If they have a good idea, explain how you will implement it into the system.

Demo Masters and Bayview Environmental also encourage our employees out in the field to stand up and be heard, especially in safety. If you are working for any of our companies as a field worker, a foreman, a superintendent, or even the warehouse delivery person, you need to be heard as well.

If anyone witnesses a coworker or a visitor at one of our job sites and they are not wearing protective gear, they need to stand up and say something. They have a right and a duty to inform that person that they need to put on the proper safety gear, whether it is safety glasses, boots, hard hat, eye protection, or whatever the project requires. They can and should speak on behalf of the entire company to get this right and to prevent an accident from happening.

This goes for anyone at any level. If a laborer sees the foreman walking around a job site and he is not wearing his safety glasses, he should get the foreman's attention and politely say, "Hey, boss, you need your safety glasses on." The only response this laborer should hear is, "Thank you. Good job."

You again don't want anyone feeling like they can't speak up and help direct where the company is planning to go. If all the employees feel they can stay true to the plan and they feel like they are a part of the plan, which they are, then why on earth would you not praise that? Why would you be against support and ideas from employees or coaches if you really want them to be a part of a plan? I can only think of a couple of words for that: insecure and immature. If that's you, grow up and embrace those around you, and you'll see that your plan will be working better soon.

8

Stay Calm When Pressure Hits

I was coaching from the booth during a Friday night football game several years ago, and I was there with another assistant coach and the offensive coordinator, who was having a very tough night. He was trying to make play calls that would catch the opposing team's defense off guard, to no avail. He was determined to run plays over and over again that just weren't working. He could not get his mind into the fact that the defense was blitzing our offensive line hard, and the quarterback did not have time to take a seven-step drop and complete a play deep down the field. He just kept on trying to prove his plays would work and wanted to go deep.

He started to get flustered and would call a play with the wrong formation, such as a left call when it should have been a right call. He started getting more and more frustrated. I said to him, "Slow down and think about why the play is not working." I explained to him that the defense was blitzing us hard, and we should slow them down. "Let's start with our cadence. We should call the play on two or three instead of always going on one. This will slow down their quick get-offs. We can also set up some screen plays and throw more to our backs. This will help keep the linebackers in check." The other assistant coach said I was right, and we could also mix it up a little bit by throwing a couple of pop passes to the tight end off a delayed release.

He looked at us with his deer-in-the-headlights look and said, "Okay." He then continued to call the same plays he was calling before and never mixed it up. He never changed the cadence either. Nope. This guy was so stubborn that he folded under the pressure and we lost the game.

Now, I'm not one to blame a lost football game on any one play or any one person. No, there's always more than one reason a game goes badly. However, this is about as close as you can get to losing a game by yourself. This guy let himself get so rattled that he lost his control. He allowed a few bad play calls to take him away from smart decision making. He allowed one or two mistakes to turn into ten or twelve.

If he had stayed calm, and if he had communicated with the other assistant coach and me, he would not have felt so much pressure. Part of the game is play calling and mixing it up. It's about working with all coaches and planning out strategies together. It is also about trying to outcoach the opponent's coach. It's the cat-and-mouse part of the game that makes coaching great.

He was trying to impress the fans with his deep passing game, and he didn't give our opponent's coaching staff any credit for studying film on his predictable offense. He did not have the maturity to remain calm and work with the other coaches in a reasonable fashion. He got lost in his own mistakes, and he caused more mistakes to be made. He should have stayed calm.

We all should note that part of this game is about the fact that players will make mistakes, even if you did have the right play call in. There will be penalties that will bring back a great play. Whatever can happen, will happen at some point. You just try and calm yourself down and reevaluate the situation and call the next play.

I was coaching a youth football game, and I was the acting head coach for this game because the official head coach could not attend for personal reasons.

I normally was the defensive coordinator for this team; however, I was asked to head up this game. I asked the offensive coordinator to keep the ball on the ground. The team we were playing that weekend had some good pass rushing defensive ends on their team, and they were big kids. The two middle linebackers were fast but not very strong. I felt our running back could handle them running straight ahead. I also told the offensive coordinator that I did not want to throw the ball deep because their defensive ends had the ability to sack our quarterback in the backfield.

The offensive coordinator's son was the team quarterback, and the first and second plays of the game, the offensive coordinator called deep pass plays, which did not work. Guess why? Yep! The defensive ends got him. I told the coach if he called another deep pass play without checking with me first, I would remove him from play calling altogether.

This tough-fought game was nearing the end, and we were up on the scoreboard 6 to 0. Our opponents had the ball with about 1 1/2 minutes left on the clock, and they were on our 4-yard line and looking to score. The offensive coordinator was getting very nervous and expressed to me several times throughout the game that my game plan for this week was hurting his son's passing stats. I told him I didn't care about stats during a game. I only look at them after a game. He continued pacing next to me as I called a corner blitz. As our cornerback came off the corner, he ran right by the tailback unblocked and sacked the opposing quarterback, which caused him to fumble the ball, and we recovered the fumble.

It was our ball with less than a minute to go, and we were on our own 5-yard line with a 6-to-0 lead. I looked at the offensive coordinator, and I said to him, "Run the ball and seal the win." Well, he decided to boost his son's stats and called a deep post pattern instead. Our quarterback was sacked in the end zone and fumbled the ball. The opposing team recovered it for a touchdown, and then they kicked the two-point conversion (in youth football, it's two points for kicking the extra point and one point for running it in), and we lost the game 6 to 8.

The biggest disaster for these kids is that this would have been their first win in nine weeks. We had the number two-ranked defense in the league and the worst offense in the league that season. This coach was making play calls to boost his son's stats instead of generating yardage and putting the team in position to win. I'm sure he wanted to win, but he should have been removed from play calling if that is the kind of decisions he makes. This coach lost his composure and became so uncontrollable that he allowed himself to create unnecessary pressure on himself, the team, and his son. This behavior will get you making bad decision after bad decision.

You must stay calm and play the game the way it is intended. It's not about you and your kid's stats. And when you think like this person, you miss the simple and the obvious. Wouldn't you rather give your son a victory for a stat than a loss with a lot of passing yards? You think better and you make fewer errors, if you just stay calm and let your mind think things through.

So many times I've watched coaches running up and down the sidelines screaming at the officials and screaming at their own players, just getting all wound up, and then make a hasty play call only to have it turn out badly, and then scream some more and create a ton of tension for their coaches and players. Then a play goes well and they are jumping up and down with joy. They applaud the fans in the stands, they praise the kids, they act like they did something brilliant, and all they really did was create confusion. Then a play goes badly and they start all over again with the childish behavior.

This uncontrolled behavior, running on high emotions then low emotions, creates havoc on your sidelines. It's this negative high-tension atmosphere that is taking away your ability to remain calm and coach with good decision making. Instead of coaching through frustration, try coaching with the mind-set that this is the cat-and-mouse part of the game, and it's a very fun part of the game, so enjoy it. Staying cool and collected will minimize the bad moments and increase the good ones.

I was the defensive coordinator for the freshman football team at Clayton Valley High School a few years back, and we were playing against my former high school, Pinole Valley. The kids were really pumped up for this game. They knew it was my old high school, and they wanted to win it for me. They were so pumped up at first that they were actually playing like crap. Pinole Valley ran the ball right down our throats on their opening drive, and after seven consecutive running plays, they were down on our 18-yard line.

I could see that our kids were gasping for air and their hands were on their hips, so I called for a time-out. As I was walking across the field toward my players, I could see the disappointment in their faces. They were a very good defensive football team, and they knew they were blowing it. They wanted this win so badly that they lost their composure, and they lost their reason for playing the game in the first place. It was not about winning the game for me because I went to high school there; it was about the competition of this game, the contact and the relationship you build with your teammates, and fighting through the challenges as a team.

As I approached the players, I told them all to huddle up. I wanted to say something. They got close, and in a very upbeat voice, I said, "Isn't this a great game? They think they are going to score, and we know they're not. Here is what we are going to do." I told my middle linebackers that the tailback for Pinole Valley was carrying the football with one hand, like the ball had a handle. "We need to strip the ball out of his hands," I said, and told the strongside backer to key the tailback, meet him in the hole, and stand him up. I told the weakside backer to go for the ball strip.

The very next play, it worked just like I had drawn it up. We recovered the football, and we stopped them from scoring on the opening drive. The kids settled in and played a great football game from that play on and went on to win 55 to 14. I believe those kids on that team who heard me that day will always remember that play, that experience, and the way I stayed calm through it.

If a screaming-type of a coach had run out there that day and started yelling at those players at that particular time, the players may have gotten overwhelmed and never recovered. They may not have won the game, especially by the margin they did win it by.

Parents are no exception to this rule about staying calm. I have seen them do some crazy things too. When I was the defensive coordinator for the Clayton Valley Pee Wee football team, the head coach had some personal problems and did not show up for practice a few times, and it was becoming more and more often that he was not there. The less he showed up, the more the other coaches stopped showing up. And on this one evening, I was coaching practice by myself. So to keep things controllable, I did a lot of scrimmaging. I'm not a big fan of a lot of scrimmaging, but this way I could coach kids up while they were in their positions.

I was organizing the scrimmage when a friend, the assistant coach on the Junior Midget team, asked me if I needed a hand. I said I could use the help, and he worked it out with his head coach and came over to help. I gave him the offense, and I took the defense. We began the scrimmage. I was moving up and down the defensive line, coaching each player one at a time. I would tell him or her the play call, and I would coach them up play-by-play, then move to the next player and do the same thing. I started with the left defensive end and moved to the right, player by player. As I got to the right tackle, I realized the left defensive end's dad was coaching his son to do something different than I just asked him to do.

We were in a 6/2 defense, and I wanted the ends to take two steps up field and then box inward toward the quarterback. The team we were playing that week ran a lot of sweeps, and I wanted to force the running back inside to our linebackers and safeties. This defensive end's dad was telling him to slant inside off the defensive tackle's rear end.

I went over to the dad and asked him not to do that. I didn't need to, but felt I should explain to him why I was coaching the way I was. He just looked at me and never said a word. Later, he was doing it again. I spoke to him one more time, and he said his son could get more tackles if I let him tackle the running back when the running back ran inside. I explained to him again that the linebackers had the inside run and the defensive ends had to be ready if they faked the dive and tossed the ball on the sweep or nobody would be there to stop it. Five minutes later, he did it again. I then got a little angry and said in a stern voice, "I'm out here doing this with just the help of the other coach, who was good enough to lend me a hand, and you are being a burden to me. Your kid is getting confused. If you really want to help, you could get out here and help me coach all the kids, not just yours."

This parent was getting frustrated by the head coach not showing up and the lack of coaching that was going on during the season with the assistant coaches also not showing up. I don't blame him for that, but if he had remained calm, and if he had offered with some of the other parents to get involved, something better may have worked out.

If I had remained calm that night also, I could have asked for the parents to get involved and could have made it a fun thing by teaching them how to coach. It could have been fun for all of us. I'm sure the kids would have liked their moms and dads helping out for a night or two.

When there is a person who is out of control and the other one can remain calm, something good may come out of it. I think I learned more that night than the dad did.

I was the go-to guy for this abatement company back in the mid-eighties. I would be the guy the company called when a project went badly, no matter where it was. I would put together a team of people I trusted, and off we would go, sometimes for a day or two, and sometimes for weeks.

This time it was off to Puerto Rico to take over a project that was loaded with embezzlement, theft, incompletion, and corruption. In addition to those things, I was to finish building a cooling tower at a power plant in Puerto Rico. I had no idea what a cooling tower was at the time. It's a very big multistory structure that cools down power stations. It works like a giant radiator. We also had a problem with the local foreman we hired in Puerto Rico, who was cheating on the payroll. They would sign in fake names of employees and claim to have fifteen people working at the project and really only had seven or eight, and they'd keep the extra payroll checks for themselves and cash them. The person the company found embezzling was removed from the project and arrested before I got there.

I brought Jay Randall with me on this trip, my longtime friend and company superintendent, along with a bilingual foreman to help us communicate once we were there. I contacted this top foreman I'd worked with before, and with him and Jay, we were set to go. These two individuals are hard working, they are excellent thinkers, they are very direct with other people, and they stay calm under pressure. These two guys are still working with me to this day.

Jay and I were sitting next to each other on the plane, and he asked me, "What are you going to do about the payroll cheats?"

I said, "I don't have a clue, but it needs to be dealt with first. And if it goes badly, it could get ugly for us."

"That's why I asked," he said.

I decided not to worry about it that much. If I relaxed and remained calm, my mind would figure it out.

About an hour before we landed in Puerto Rico, the idea came to me. We had already talked to the two Puerto Rican foremen several days earlier about picking us up at the airport, so I was going to meet with the foremen there. They were there waiting for us as planned, and to my surprise, they spoke pretty good English. I asked to speak to them in private, and they agreed and went to a corner and sat down. I told them I knew about the phony employees and I knew that they kept the checks. I also told them as long as I was there running the project, the fake checks were going to be eliminated. I also asked them how much they were making an hour. They told me they were getting $12 an hour. "Okay, look," I said. "If you two agree that I will run the time sheets and we eliminate the fake checks, I'll increase your pay to $25 an hour."

They said, "Yes, Mr. Don," and the company saved hundreds of dollars an hour by eliminating the fake payroll checks.

A week later, we were getting close to completion, and I was not sure if we would make the deadline. The job was tough, and it was hard getting the locals to show up every day. One day we had ten guys, the next day we would have four guys, and the schedule was coming to an end. I went back to our makeshift office, and I started a new completion plan. I figured out what was left to be completed and how many men I would need to get it done for each day. I needed the full crew of ten workers per day for the next six days, but how was I going to get the workers to show up? With that in the back of my mind I also needed to get the equipment back home so I asked Jay to help me out, and he called a shipping company to get some pricing on sending back the tools, equipment, and our Toyota pickup truck. He came back to me with the pricing, which was about $12,000 and then it came to me.

All the pieces were there. We had some gang boxes, some minor materials, Skil saws, some other hand tools, and the truck. This stuff was all worth about $4,800 collectively. Why pay $12,000 to get it home?

I went to the two Puerto Rican foremen and told them I had another deal to discuss with them. I told them they could keep the truck and all the tools and remaining supplies if we met the deadline and if they could keep the needed ten workers on the job every day to get it done. They said, "Yes, Mr. Don." The project was completed on time, and I signed over the pink slip as promised.

Pressure in your everyday life, as well as in business and coaching, is something all of us have to handle. If you control your emotions and calm yourself down, you will find that you can ease yourself through the pressure and come out successfully through it all.

Saturday mornings, my wife Leslie and I get our cup of coffee and read the newspaper together. It is something I look forward to. On this one particular Saturday morning, Leslie said to me while she was reading the paper, "Hey, look. Mark McCullah's picture is in the paper." Mark is our very good friend who happens to be a Contra Costa County Battalion Fire Chief.

The picture in the newspaper showed Mark talking to a distraught-looking firefighter. In the background of the picture was a mangled-up vehicle that looked as if it had rolled over several times, an ambulance, and a couple of paramedics attending to the crash victim. The crash victim was in very bad shape. My wife said to me, "Look at Mark in this picture. He is smiling. I wonder why he is smiling." With your first look at the picture, it would appear that he was inappropriately smiling at a horrific crash scene. However,

I know this guy, and he is very professional and would never take something like this lightly.

I told her to look again at the picture. In the picture, the chief was looking directly into the face of the young distraught firefighter. The firefighter was on one knee and getting comforted by the battalion chief. I told her I'd bet the young firefighter got a little overwhelmed and Mark picked up on the pressure this firefighter was having.

A couple of days later, I ran into Mark, and I asked him about the picture in the paper. He said he had not seen it and really never cared what was in the paper. I asked him why he was smiling at the scene, and he told me the young firefighter had arrived at the scene a short time before he did. When the young firefighter came over to the chief, he told him about some of the gross details of the victim in the wreck. The chief realized the firefighter could pass out or get sick. He also knew the pressure could get to the firefighter and could cause a scene or get somewhat embarrassing for the young firefighter. Mark started talking to the firefighter about some of his interests and tried to make the moment light, to give the firefighter time to collect himself.

By the battalion chief staying calm and easing the tension that was surfacing at the scene, he was able to get the firefighter to come to grips with his thoughts. After a short period of time, they were all back to making good decisions to help others.

Staying calm and controlling your highs and lows of emotions will benefit you a great deal in handling pressure, whether you are on the sidelines or in the boardroom.

9

Sharing Your Experiences

I've often said that coaching is the next best thing to playing. At some point, you can no longer play the sport that you have loved for so many years, and yet you just can't stay away from it. You may have even played it a little longer than you should have, but you were willing to play it until they came out with a large hook to snag you away and told you not to come back. Maybe what they meant was not to come back as a player. Maybe you could come back as a coach.

I was a very good football player in Pop Warner youth and in high school at Pinole Valley. I was like most kids back then. If you had some success on the football field, you would get letters by head coaches from colleges with a request for you to consider their school as one of the potential colleges on your list. You would then check your grade point average to see if you could even get in to that college. If you were an exceptional player, the college head coaches went after you hard. They would know about your grade point average, and they would find out what they could about your family background. They would look at whatever angle they could to get at you to see if you would be a good fit in their program. Now it is more evolved with the Internet, state rankings, nationwide player rankings, Nike camps, high school combines, and I'm sure much more.

Anyway, I did not get that kind of attention, mainly because I never had the grades to be taken seriously. If my grade point average was one point lower I think they would have put me in a padded room someplace. I was (and still am) a terrible speller. History and geography? Really? Who needs this? However, I did have good people skills, which showed up as the class clown, and I had the football credentials to play anywhere.

I was All League and All Eastbay, on the Dream Team, and had a state record twenty-five quarterback sacks my senior year, five of them in the North Coast Championship game alone. I also started at tailback for that championship game because our All League running back broke his tailbone during the playoff game the week before. Pinole Valley won that championship game 6 to 0 against Washington High of Fremont.

With my size of five feet, nine inches and 165 pounds my senior year, there weren't a lot of college coaches looking for me to play outside linebacker as I did in high school, but some did like me at strong safety. Still, nobody liked my grade point average of 2.5.

When I had been out of high school for about ten years, I was playing golf at Richmond Country Club in Richmond, California, at a local fundraiser. I was playing in a group with my former high school coaches. One of them asked me if I had remembered the coaches from Texas A&M coming out for a visit. I said, "Kind of," and he said, "Well, back then I did not see a reason to tell you the story, but you can handle it now, so here is the story. The A&M coaches called the school and asked for some tape on you, so I sent them a couple of good ones. They later called and asked if they could have a visit. They were coming out our way on a recruiting tour and had some kids in mind at other schools in the area and were still unsure about you. They thought, why not come by and meet the kid to finalize their choices? A few weeks later, they came out to meet with you and me. We met early because you and I had the early P.E. class called A-Period and you were my teacher's aide in that class. Well, the A&M coaches wanted to squeeze you into their busy schedule, and early was good for them too. We met for about fifteen minutes, and as far as you know, they never called again."

Coach went on to say that the A&M coaches did call him a week later and said they were not interested in me. They said I looked a lot bigger on tape than I was in person. Coach in his own words told me he said to the A&M coach, "Well, Coach, I know he is not very big, but he is a very tough kid, has won many personal awards, and he is very intimidating when he steps on the football field around here." Coach gave me the A&M coach's response in his weak attempt at a Texas accent and said, "Well, Coach, he might scare some folks around there, but he ain't gonna scare the hell out of nobody in Texas."

I had letters from UC Davis and Hayward State, had a tryout with San Francisco State, and heard from a few Ivy League schools. Sure, I'm going there with my 2.5 GPA. I signed up at San Francisco State and played there for a few months, but was not focused in really taking schoolwork seriously. I thought my ability to play football would handle everything. The coaches would like me and somehow get a tutor to do my homework for me or something like that. I soon came to realize that I'm just not good enough of a football player to have everything handed to me. Don't get me wrong here. I worked very hard at football, and I spent a lot of time staying in shape, but I mailed it in when it came to schoolwork, something I will always regret, but I have moved on and forgave myself. Without any parental guidance, I was left to make decisions on my own and made them the best I knew how. You stand by them and support them if they work or learn from them and try not to repeat them if they don't.

My father left when I was three years old, and the stepfather I had would not in any way be considered a role model. He had drinking problems and never really held a job for more than a few years. My mother, who was always supportive of anything I did, just did not know much about college, tuitions, or dealing with college football programs, so I was on my own and not liking where I was headed. I decided to end my football dreams and focus on something else I was really good at: working. So I packed up and went to work.

Maybe these are the reasons I'm so passionate about helping kids through this game. These are the things I think about most when I'm coaching. Not every kid who plays football comes from a broken home or is so poor you want to shower them in pity, but if you're fortunate enough to be coaching football and teaching kids the right things in life and you happen to come across a kid or two who need someone with experiences like yours and you can help them make good choices, that is something you will take with you forever. That is a big part of why you should want to coach, so you can help steer kids in the right direction. I call it molding the minds of the youth! Plus as an added bonus, you get another opportunity to stay close to the game of football.

A good coach will use everything he or she has when it comes to reaching the kids. They use their shortcomings, their experiences good or bad, and maybe even some of their regrets to help their kids and yours reach the dreams that they may or may not have reached for themselves.

I think it is okay to be a selfish coach if you are selfish about helping kids achieve their own goals, and if you as a coach are selfish in a way that you won't allow bad coaches to alter your way of doing what is right for the betterment of these kids.

If you're the kind of person who gets satisfaction from helping kids reach their goals, if you take pride in helping kids with schoolwork so they could get a better grade point average, if you tell the kids about your accomplishments and elaborate on your regrets, then you need to be a coach. Combine the things above with your football knowledge, and you will be asking yourself, "Why am I not coaching?"

I hate to see the opportunities being lost by some coaches. They don't see the position that they are in. They don't see that they really can reach kids in a positive manner. They sometimes see it as a difficult task because a kid might be a nuisance, might be too small, might not be very athletic, or maybe the kid's parents are idiots. They don't see what they are missing and they don't realize they are coaching for the wrong reasons. They don't see that they will never find real happiness in coaching, at least not as much as they could. They will see some highs and some lows as their emotions take over from a win or a loss, but they will never find the real joy in coaching. They simply just do not realize how lucky they are to help create these young adults.

I always felt great pride seeing these young players develop into nice young men and women. I love it when I cross paths with a former player in a store, or when passing by at the park, they come up to me and tell me all about what they have been doing with their jobs or college or whatever they are into at the time. I like to listen to them and look into their faces as they explain it to me because they sometimes explain it with excitement, as if I'm their long-lost dad and they are seeking my approval.

I remember a couple of varsity players I had the pleasure of coaching at Clayton Valley; I remember many more, of course, but I remember these two because they showed up for spring practice their senior year and were not in the best shape I've seen them in. I asked them what they had been doing. They told me that they did a little partying over the summer but would not have a problem working it off. They did put in some effort and were always natural athletes, but I could tell they were clowning around too much and taking everything for granted.

I saw the two of them joking around during one practice and I went over to them during the next break and asked to speak to both of them. I said, "Look. You two have the talent to play football in college, and this is your last chance to prove it to everyone. Now, I want you guys to stop the partying and the clowning around and focus on yourselves. Don't blow this opportunity that you guys have." I also said, "Don't do this for me, and don't do it for your parents or even for the school. Just do it for yourselves." And finally I said, "Why don't you stop the partying for twelve months and devote twelve months to getting yourselves into shape to win a four-year scholarship to play football somewhere? Can't you give up one year in exchange for four?"

Well, they did do a pretty good job of it, and they did come back in shape and got to pursue their dreams. One went on to play middle linebacker at Kansas, and the other was a safety at Army. I'm not saying I had anything to do with their success. They may have gotten there anyway because they were good athletes, but as a coach, I made sure they knew their options, and I made sure they were aware of a path that needed to be played out in order to accomplish their dreams. The path I missed.

There is always a great need for more good coaches. These football programs can't survive without good coaching. Go to your local football program and ask to sign up your kid and ask to help coach. If you don't have a kid who wants to play, go and coach anyway. You will be proud of the positive impressions you can make on someone's life. Interview the coaches you are working for and discuss how they are currently helping kids and how you can help maintain a positive place for kids and the sport of football. Let's continue to weed out the coaches who are not in it for the right reasons.

I remember my younger son Blake was a good football player and a very hard worker. Blake spent the first few years playing on a team that I did not coach. I was coaching high school and my older son Nick's team at the Midget level. Blake was in the Junior Pee Wees, and the coaching staff there was pretty good. I started noticing that Blake was often saying that he was not big enough to play certain positions and could not start because he was not big enough.

I would always tell him that you don't have to be big to play this game because there are a lot of different positions to play. A really big player might not be a good cornerback, but he might be a good lineman. A small player might not be a good linebacker but might be a good running back. And besides that, he was a very good player because he was aggressive and had heart. I also told him many times not to worry about it, but it was sticking in his head because that is what his coaches were telling him. He was becoming confused as to where he may or not play.

The next year, he moved up to the Pee Wees, and I signed up to coach there so I could be with him. With positive influences from me and the other coaches, he started playing much better. He regained his confidence and became a good player for us at defensive end that year.

There is always a potential problem in coaching if you don't watch what you say to the kids, mainly in youth programs. If you tell a kid that he or she can't do something or you give them a hurtful nickname, you could mess them up in the head. They all want to be accepted, and they all want to be important. They need to know they are a part of the team. You as the coach are never to participate in the game-playing or adding pressure to the kids; that is just criminal in my book. They believe what their coaches tell them, and they will live with it for a long time.

Even if you don't think you are being negative, you still need to be careful. It is very important to be careful when you speak to these young players when you are their coach, because what you say and how you say it could affect that person for a long time.

I have talked with friends about writing this book and about the positive influence I'm hoping it will have on existing coaches as well as new ones coming in. They have expressed some concern and have asked me to explain why a coach would play a number two kid over the better-playing number one kid. What possible reason would a coach have for doing that? I'm going to explain it here: The positive reason for that would be because maybe player number one was getting a little big-headed and thinking he or she was all that, and the coach felt a punishment for a game or two was in order to teach the player that this is a team sport and no single player can win on their own. Basically, punishing the better player.

The best way to confirm that explanation is in two ways: First, go and ask the coach why the better kid is not playing. Second, ask yourself, "What kind of decisions has this coach made before?" If he is pretty consistent about making fair decisions, and you have always felt he has been fair with the kids in the past, then he probably deserves the benefit of the doubt that he is doing it again in this situation. However, if he is the type of coach who has a history of being mean, yelling, controlling kids or parents, or having an unexplainable character, then he may have other reasons as to why he would not play a better player over a lesser player.

Some coaches simply cannot evaluate talent. They really think one kid is better than another, no matter how many people tell them differently. Some coaches are so arrogant that they want to be the coach who found the diamond in the rough, the kid no one else could find, and play the kid over many others. Some, of course, play a kid because it is his own kid or the assistant coach's. Sometimes, a coach will choose to play one kid over another even though their talents are equal because one may be a senior and the other a junior. In any case, you should question why, especially if the coach has a history of making poor choices or is known for being unfair. Parents and players should never forget that these programs are there for their enjoyment and are not there for some coach with a huge ego to take over and manipulate it.

The important thing to remember here is that most youth and high school coaches are amateurs; so are the officials, and so are the people on the boards of these youth programs. If they were really awesome, they would be in college or the pros. Not that there is anything wrong with being an amateur. What I'm pointing out here is that it just means that they might be doing the best they know how, and you don't have to be so critical or judgmental. However, you do have the right to question them and maybe offer some help, and you can follow your resources if need be.

What we need is more good coaches who can see that working with the parents and the kids of their community is a great reward, and the friendship they can make will last a long time. With all the great, positive, fun things there are in coaching, there can be some negative things that will last a long time too. Avoid the negative reaction by getting into coaching with a plan to be fair to everyone and a plan to mentor and be a positive leader for the kids. You will be surprised by the amount of future friends and young adults you will get to know over the years.

Demo Masters has three superintendents, and I often remind them to do the right thing when dealing with their coworkers. I remind them never to forget that they had bosses over them before and they should look back on who motivated them the most. Was it the mean, stubborn bosses they had who made them want to work better, or was it the nice, respectful bosses who got them going? I remind them of it because I want them to lean on their own experiences. I want them to be the type of supervisor they wanted to work for, someone who is fair and respectful and not weak or a pushover. One who is simply fair and sticks to policies that have been agreed to.

They should strive to be leaders with the company's principles and the company's ethics, because these types of leaders will have people working hard for them even after they leave the job site. They won't have to wonder if work is being accomplished when they are not there to watch. The leaders below them will want to work hard for the superintendent because they feel they will share in the credit with the superintendent.

Not the same for the mean, stubborn boss. He will see people working hard when he is there, and he won't see the people not giving a crap after he leaves because they know he will keep any and all credit, should there be any.

Whether you are coaching or the superintendent of a construction company, treat people as you would want to be treated. It's the right thing to do and your best plan to get a task completed in your favor.

The same fundamental planning will take you far in business as well. I have been a business owner since 1993 and have been fortunate that during the past several years, the economy has been pretty good and keeping hold of our employees was easy. However, my partners and I are not waiting for the economy to create change for us. We know we will be facing some tough times for our business in the near future because of the California budget issues and the nationwide problems we are about to face. So we are now working on revising our business plan in order to keep our hard-working employees employed. We feel it is our duty to remain focused, for their families and ours. While most companies are trying to hold on, we have grown and diversified our business with well-thought-out planning.

Just like in coaching, you need to reevaluate your plan as things change. You need to reevaluate as if it was part of the original plan all along, because it should be. Plan B is just that: Reevaluating the plan if plan A needs to be altered.

Discover the problem and address it. If it's a sales problem, evaluate it and make some calm, well-thought-out changes, changes that will address the short-term, immediate problems and changes that will remain in place as a permanent policy to avoid a repeat of the same problem. If it's an operations problem, same thing. Evaluate the source. Take a calm approach, and make some well-thought-out changes, changes that will address the short-term, immediate problem and changes that will remain in place as a permanent policy to avoid a repeat of the same problem.

It's not the problem that is critical here. It's your ability to stay calm and remain thoughtful to the needs of the company. You don't want to spread alarm to those around you. Panic is not an option, and neither is bad decision making. When the crisis hits you, you get one chance to show leadership and instill confidence in the employees around you. If you are showing a different kind of change every other week, you will lose the confidence of your employees, and they could jump ship, leaving you without long-term, skilled people you have had for some time.

People will do what they have to do when things get bad, and they will remember how you handled things during that time. We as Americans must always believe that a crisis that comes our way is temporary. We have always overcome hard times, and we have always faced our problems head on. This is no different; however, it will not fix itself. We as leaders of our companies need to stay thoughtful, and we must think short- and long-term and make confident decisions.

I was going through this a little bit with one of my partners. He started to get caught up in the numbers (jobs that made money, jobs that didn't make money, revenues coming in, revenues that were projected to come in, etc.) and not spending enough time evaluating the numbers for accuracy. He would use the numbers as if they were the Bible.

Now, I also believe in the numbers, and you definitely need to see and review them, but I don't list it up there with the Bible, not until they have been evaluated. There are too many questions. Did the numbers get reviewed for project completion? Did the numbers get reviewed for potential change orders? Did the project finish on time? Was the original budget set up correctly? Have all costs been accounted for? Are there any costs that won't be used? The numbers are to be used as a tool to alert you that a project may be heading in the wrong direction and the project may need to be evaluated for accuracy, and once a project has been evaluated, it needs to have a plan for correction. No question, early evaluation of the numbers is a very important tool to avoid big-time trouble, but they should be seen as a tool until the numbers have been confirmed and then they can be seen as the Bible. Then if needed, the project may be reevaluated.

Most of my experience was in operations, and I had built successful programs for three companies during my career up to that point, and I don't believe in making changes every week because some new numbers come in. If you are proactive in running the projects from the beginning and you have a feel for the project, then look at the numbers as a tool.

Construction companies should monitor their projects by using their own experiences and the experiences of their field superintendents and their foremen in conjunction with the reported numbers. Once you have all the information you can collect, along with the experience you and your company employees have, you'll find yourself in position to create a great plan for each and every one of your projects.

These are some tough times coming, and my partners and I will continue to remain calm and thoughtful. We may disagree about how we will accomplish our goals, but we will work together because we all have the same principles and we all share the same respect for each other and our employees, who have been with us for so long. We will continue with our company plans, and we will continue to find ways to keep our businesses going as we always have: through calm and thoughtful thinking.

10

Giving Support

Nothing is more heartbreaking than to see a young player looking up in the stands to see if their parents are there to watch them perform in a game. It is absolutely unacceptable to me when a parent drops off their kid at practice as if the coaches are there to babysit for a couple of hours while the parents are off doing whatever it is that they do. It would be inconceivable for me to ever do that. These kids want and need to impress you. They want to impress their coaches too, but for different reasons. Your kids need your support, your love, and your approval. It is that simple.

Support is also needed for the team. Can you help the coach? Hold a stopwatch and record players' timing? Set up cones? Work the snack shack? Help out being the team mom? Just offering any kind of help is much-needed support. Even if all you can do is show up at practice and be ready to help do whatever is asked of you.

Don't look at it as if you're being punished. There are some great things that can come out of being involved. You can build friendships with other parents and get a better understanding of the coaches. My wife and I have made several very close friends through being involved. There is nothing wrong with being a part of your child's life or helping your community, is there? In fact, it's your responsibility to do so.

Let me mention exactly what kind of support it is that we are looking for: it's the positive kind, the good sportsmanship kind.

Sometimes, you will find a parent who loves to scream from the stands, "What kind of call was that?" or "You call yourself an official?" or "Come on, Coach. Put my kid in so we can win." Even the old classic, "Hey, Ref. I'll double what they are paying you." Those parents really are not helping. This is not supporting the team; in fact, it is distracting the team, and it's making them look like a fool.

That type of behavior is embarrassing to your kid also. Believe me when I tell you, your kid is embarrassed when you do that. I'm talking firsthand here. I have never been on the sidelines during a football game or a baseball game, for that matter, and heard a parent screaming from the bleachers down to the field of play and then have that parent's kid say to me, "Boy, that's my dad. Look at him go. Isn't he the best supporter of the team?" Never happens!

Remind me of the last time you went to one of your kid's games and after the game was over you went home and said, "Boy, that was a good game, and I really enjoyed it when Mr. Smith stood up and started screaming at the coaches and showing how angry he can get at the officiating. That just topped the night. I hope I get to sit by him next week."

Did you ever say that? Did you ever enjoy that? I'm guessing no. That is not the support we need. We need real support from the parents.

If you remain active in your kid's life, nobody loses. I know it is hard when you and your spouse work, and I know it's hard to find the time when you have other children who are young also, but they are yours. These kids are yours, and they need you there.

Time will move very fast, and you won't believe it until it passes you by. Just like many of you, we were told by parents whose kids were grown that we should pay closer attention to our kids because they will grow up before you know it and you will miss your opportunity to be a part of their lives. I spent a lot of time with my kids, more than most, and I still feel like I missed some of it.

Do more. Find the time to be a part of your kids' lives. Spend more time helping them see the life's lessons that are being taught in sports, and show them that your support is there for them throughout a lifetime.

I was coaching the Pee Wees one year with a friend I had met through coaching. This guy was the head coach, and I was his defensive coordinator and assistant head coach. His coaching style was not the best, but he did have a big heart and was looking to make the kids better players. We had a losing record at this point in the season, and Coach was not making too many friends with the parents, mostly because of the losing record. To the defense of the parents, we had better players than our record showed, and the offense was struggling to get points.

Coach was having some trouble with his job and I think some trouble at home, and he started missing some practices. Missing the practices was not the problem for me. It was more about not knowing if he was showing up to run practice or not.

Because I did not know, I was unprepared the first few times. I showed up to run my drills for the defense and realized I would need to run the coach's offense also. After a couple of days of that, I got ready to do both, and if he showed up, fine. If not, I was ready to just step in and organize the other assistant coaches and run things.

One night when the coach did not show up again, I decided to put in a couple of new offensive plays. I was thinking for some time we could use a few plays that would take advantage of the outside speed we had, so I put them in. After some tweaking, they looked really good in practice.

On the next practice day, the head coach showed up, and I went over the new offensive plays that we put in the night before, and again, they looked really good. He got upset that I was changing his offense. I explained to him I was not trying to change his offense, I was just adding a couple of plays that could add some balance to the offense in an effort to get the offense moving the ball.

I also told him that I understood he was having some problems with his personal life that he needed to handle first. I would run the program as he wanted but was insistent that he look at the plays I put in with an open mind. He agreed to take another look. After our conversation, he realized that the plays were something we could use, and more importantly, he realized I was supporting his personal needs and doing what I thought was best for the team.

That next Saturday, we played a very good game against a very good team but lost again 6 to 0. After the game was over, the coaches and I walked across the field and shook hands with the opposing coaches, then turned around and picked up our gear. As I was headed to the parking lot, a small group of parents from our team came over to me and said that they were going to the president of the board to ask to have the head coach removed and they wanted my support. I asked them, "If the coach goes, then who will run the team?"

"Well, we thought you would," they said.

I told them, "This person is volunteering his time, and I'm aware that he has had some personal troubles and missed some practices, but this coach has your kids at heart. He has taught them good football skills, and he has been volunteering his time for several years. I know he has not won many games this year, but that's not a good reason to ask for him to be removed." I told them I would not be a part of him being removed and I would leave if he were removed. "I'm going to support the fact that he is good for the kids. Be a little patient with him, and don't get wrapped up in the winning and losing of it all. Look more at the kids. They are better football players now, and they will be ready to move up next year." I also said that there was room for some of these parents to get involved and help. The head coach could use the support. They did not want to be that kind of help, I found out, when they rejected my offer.

Support has different meanings, I'm sure, to different people. What is it really? It can be money, it can be services, or it can be praying. I'm sure you have your own definition.

My very good friend Kurt Crigger always speaks highly of the support he always got from his father. His father was always supporting him with his sports and personal decisions that came his way. He still speaks of the support he got from his father, even now after his recent passing. I was not fortunate enough to have that. Kurt is very lucky in that respect. He told me once that his view of support is being there for someone you care about, like his father was for him. So for me, I think it's knowing that you really want to see other people succeed so much that you are willing to do more than just say it.

There was trouble on another project, and the company I was working for called me in to handle it. This time, the project was for a school district in Las Vegas, and I needed to go there immediately to check it out. This was my third year in a row going to Las Vegas to bail out a project for this company. The good news was I had it down: the hotels, the per diem money, the vendors, and how to control the crew, in regard to the nightlife and them gambling all their per diem money away. I went out there and evaluated the problems and put together the same crew as the two previous years. Why not? We always got the job done.

The owner of the company told me that I was to leave with my crew the following week. We had always stayed at the hotel I set up for a couple of reasons: #1. It was cheap, and it included free meals at the hotel's buffets. #2. We would be able to have two guys to a room. Most of the other places were so expensive that we would have three or four in one room.

I wanted my crew comfortable at all times. I understood they were away from their homes and working on a difficult project. The last thing I needed was the crew wanting to go home or not wanting to go on the next job assignment. They knew I would set them up with good accommodations, and I knew they would work hard.

It is always difficult to keep your crew focused on out-of-town projects, especially when you are in Las Vegas. That is why I handpicked these guys, and that is why I gave them their per diem money in small amounts every two days. If I were to give them all their money for the week, they would gamble it away and start borrowing money from me, something I learned during year number one there in Las Vegas.

We had this trip down. We had the crew. We had the hotel, two men to a room. We had the per diem set up in a controlled manner. Plus the vendors were on board with the discounts. Everything was set up, and my crew of seven plus myself flew out. We arrived at our hotel lobby right on time. I asked my right-hand man, Mike Morelli, to hold the guys where they stood so I could get us signed into the hotel.

As I was walking over to the check-in counter, I heard my name being called out. When I looked over, it was the operations manager of the company I was working for. I said, "Hello. What are you doing here?" He said he had been there for a week, and he wanted to give me some support on the project. He also said he had been looking for a place for my crew to stay. I told him I had it worked out already and I had a system that was right for this town. He also added he hired a project manager to oversee the project. He introduced me to him, someone I had never met.

I said, "Hello. I'm sure you are a nice guy, but I don't need this kind of support." I then told the operations manager that I was sent there to run this project, as I had in the past, with my handpicked crew. He told me he had been there for a week and found some kitchenettes for us to stay in. He said they were nice and you could get four people to a room. He told me the cost of the rooms and said it was the best deal around. I explained to him that the rooms I had were cheaper and it was two guys to a room, plus with the kitchenettes, he would have to give each guy additional per diem money. I further explained that I had been doing this for two years, and I had saved the company money every year doing it. Plus if he had done his job in the first place, the company would not need to send me there to fix it.

I told him it was important to stay with what I had set up because the project couldn't afford wasteful spending if we wanted to finish the project within the budget. He tried to pull rank on me by saying he was over me and he would make all the calls from here on out. "Will you support me?" I replied with my right hand circling in the air to Mike Morelli as I said, "Mike, pack them up. We are going home."

The operations manager asked me to stop. "Let's call the office," he said, "and talk with one of the owners."

We called, and he explained his position to the owner, and then handed me the phone as if to say I told you so. The owner said, "We were just looking to give you some support over there." I explained how things had worked out the past two years and why they wanted me and my crew back there for a third time. They did not call anyone else because they knew we would get it done and they also knew that we did not just finish the project, we did it saving money. I then said, "If you really want to support me, buy these guys a plane ticket home." They were gone later that day.

They were not out there to give me support. They wanted to be a part of fixing the project without really taking any responsibility for it. If they wanted to support me, they would have called me and let me know they had been there for a week already. They would have asked what they could do to help me. Just showing up and trying to surprise me with what they thought were savings was no help at all.

The operations manager maybe meant well, but he should have called me before they went there and discussed what my plan was and asked if there was any way they could help to save even more. I would have liked that kind of support.

11

Camp Concord for Moms

When the new coaching staff and I took over the Concord High School football program, we understood the Concord community was losing interest in the football program. Who could blame them? The school had only won a few games in the past four seasons. The new head coach had some really good ideas to get the players involved, he brought in some great conditioning drills that the kids thought were fun, and he was a very good motivator. The kids got involved in the fundraisers, and they worked hard at building the confidence back into the community. As good as this was going, I still wanted to bring in more excitement and involvement from the parents.

I had teenage kids myself, and my wife and I know what it's like to get them to talk to you after a practice. I coached my kids, so I did not need to ask them how practice went. But every single night, when my wife first laid eyes on one of her sons, she would ask in her loving voice, "How was practice, sweetie?" And every night, she would get the same answer from them: "Good." That was it. "Good."

Now, my wife is not the normal wife. No, she knows football as well as most of my male friends. She was brought up around it, and she has been around it with me. When she was a young girl, one of her best friends was Kristi Anderson, whose father is George Anderson, the former trainer for the Oakland and Los Angeles Raiders. When she was in high school, she had the pleasure of watching me play. (That was a joke.) Kidding aside, she was a high school cheerleader, and she has sat by my side watching football for about thirty years. She can call a penalty during a play before the referee throws a flag. "That's holding right there," she would say. "Isn't that a horse collar?" she might ask. And then the referee throws a flag, and she would say, "I thought so." I've taught her over the years to pay attention to where the flag comes from, you know, what part of the field it came from. Was the flag thrown toward the line of scrimmage? Or was it thrown in the backfield? If it was in the backfield, you could probably assume holding or roughing the passer or hands to the face, but you probably won't see pass interference or face guarding. Those flags you would see in a different area on the field. This is how she got so good at it. She understands the game, and she looks for what might happen in that area of play. So she never did let the kids off on the "Good" answer. She knew the coaches, and she knew the game, and these kids opened up and gave her the football information she was seeking.

That was how I came up with the idea to create Camp Concord for Moms. My wife was enjoying football because she understood how the game was to be played. She also knew the players' positions and what the players' duties were on the field. If I could get the moms to at least understand the position that their own child was playing (or supposed to be playing) when they took the field, the moms may enjoy the game more and have better dialog with their child when he or she came home from practice or after a game. I also wanted to get the moms to know one another. If the moms knew each other and liked each other, they may want to work with each other. Any football program needs hardworking, helpful moms and dads, and if they are called upon to help out, you will find less hesitation from them if they knew they could call upon four or five other moms that they have met or already know.

I'm afraid that a lot of head coaches at the youth or high school level who are in the position to run a program that requires the use of volunteers really don't understand or don't care that the volunteer has a full life going on too. These volunteers have jobs and a home to manage, help their kids with homework, and pay bills; some are running businesses, some travel a lot with their work, besides the fact they may have other kids in other sports that require them to do volunteer work.

They want to help but can't always do it alone. They need help from other volunteers. As head coach, you should realize that you need the volunteers, and you should involve the volunteers with as little impact as possible. You chose to be the head coach because this is what you wanted to do. This is your dream to run the program, so don't just dump your duties on the volunteers. Organize your needs. Put one of your assistant coaches on every program that requires the use of volunteers so the volunteers have a designated person to work with. You need to attend most if not all of these programs from time to time. Remember chapter 5, "Let Them Be Proud Too." It's important for you as the leader to be seen by the volunteers and for you to let them know you know who they are and what they are doing.

The head coach must be sympathetic to the fact that their volunteers have a life and they are needed at home too. Do what you can to help the volunteers know they have other volunteers to help them. Maybe you can set up your own Camp Concord for Moms and get your volunteers to meet the other volunteers.

I discussed my plan with the coaching staff and asked if they would participate in the program. They, of course, said they would. This was a great group of coaches, and they were all for whatever it would take to make the program successful. I hope the head coach really appreciated what he had there: some really good people and very talented coaches.

I met with the team mom and told her we were going to set up a program called Camp Concord for Moms. The program would require all the players' moms to meet on the practice field one Saturday morning. We would do this sometime during spring practices.

The moms would show up in their sweatpants, tennis shoes, and sweatshirts, ready to participate in a scheduled practice. The moms would all gather up, and the coaches would introduce themselves. "Hi. I'm Coach Howell and I am the running backs coach." If your son or daughter was a running back, then you would go with me to my practice area, where you would participate in my running backs drills. You would be doing exactly what your kids did during a normal day of practice. You also got to learn what your child's responsibilities were, what they saw when running through the line of scrimmage, what it looked like when a linebacker was running at them, and so on. You learned exactly what your little high school football player was doing out there and what they were supposed to be doing out there. You met their coaches, and you had a better understanding of what your kid was doing the next time you watched them play in a game.

After the practice was over, we split the moms up, and we had a little flag football game, Green versus Gold. Then we finished it off with a catered BBQ lunch hosted by my wife and served by the players. Another cool thing about it all was they had fun meeting and playing with the other moms. They became passionate about the team, and they became part of the program. Moms later came to me and said that they talked about it with their coworkers the whole next week. They really had fun.

Bringing your players, your coaches, your players' parents, administrators, and the volunteers that you have working with you into the fun should be top priority when setting up a new program or revitalizing an old one. It's never too late to give an old program some fun, positive changes so that everyone in the community can enjoy it too.

If you are a high school principal or the athletic director and are overseeing the football program, and the program is not running the way that you or your community may want it to be, then consider some changes. Ask your head coach to work with you on some of the changes I described in this book. If they won't change or don't believe they need to change, then I would be a little more persistent in the next conversation or even look to replace the head coach. I'm not talking about wins and losses. I'm talking about running a football program that teaches kids the most up-to-date football techniques, one that is run with good ethics and principles, and one that includes community involvement. I promise the program can't miss if you're implementing the right football fundamentals, and your coaching staff teaches with good ethics and principles, and the community is behind the program; positive things will happen and wins will come.

With your coaches on board, start looking to get everyone involved. Bring in some local businesses. You often remember the local businesses when it's time for fundraisers, but they may not be on your invited list for a little fun. How about picking a local business once a week and give out a couple of field passes to them? How about inviting one of your local sports writers to one of your pasta feeds? What's wrong with getting the newspaper on your side? Bring everyone in if you can. You might have a jazz band at your school. How about letting them perform during a home game at halftime? Have someone introduce the water polo team before one game and the tennis team at the next one. Get everyone involved, I mean everyone you can. Introduce yourself and give out a field pass to your city mayor, your county supervisor, or your fire chief.

These are free things that any program will benefit from. It doesn't cost your program a single penny to say a few nice words and let someone stand on your sidelines. The rewards could be big when it's time to ask for some support at your fundraisers. How about the mayor saying a few words at the crab feed this year? Or the local businesses donating a few nice items for the auction table? Maybe the local paper will mention the crab feed for you in the paper as a donation. I think you could feel pretty safe about asking the water polo coach or the tennis coach if they could mention the fundraiser to their team's parents, don't you? After all, you did introduce them and announced their playing schedule at one of your games. Getting people involved just makes sense. Let them all in, let them all help, and let them enjoy the game like we do.

I was asked to meet with my supervisors regarding another project that was heading down the tubes. The company had a contract with Pacific Gas and Electric Company out at their Moss Landing facility near Watsonville, California. The project was in its third week of a five-week contract, and their supervisors reported that our crews on the project could not possibly finish in the two weeks remaining. They believed it would take four more weeks to complete the project at the rate it was being handled. They also reported many safety concerns, lack of attention from our general foreman, fighting between our foremen, and poor work practices.

This project consisted of one general foreman, four foremen, and a crew of about twenty-five laborers. The company asked me to go down there immediately and assess the problems. I asked to bring along my close friend and the company's respected project superintendent, Jay Randall. They agreed, and I called Jay right away. I told Jay about the problems as I knew them to be and explained we would be in for a long night but should be home the following day. Without time to pack an overnight bag, we just headed down to the PG&E facility with the clothes on our backs.

I asked my supervisors not to contact anybody from the crew down there. I wanted Jay and I to get there and see how the project was running without anyone trying to correct his or her wrongdoings or hiding something from me before we arrived. I did not see any reason to contact the general foreman, the foremen, or anyone else there, for that matter. PG&E has always had the best people around managing and running their projects, and safety always came first (and still does) on their projects, so if they were calling the owners of the company I was working for, it was serious. That is why I wanted to see things for myself, as they were. If anybody knew I was coming, they could cover things up; I would never know if it was our general foreman not doing his duties, or maybe the foremen were not listening to the general foreman, or maybe the laborers were not following the program that had been laid out. There are many things that could be the problem here, and I wanted to see it firsthand. I wasn't trying to be sneaky by coming down as a surprise. I just wanted to capture the project in its existing state.

We arrived at the facility around 8:30 that night and walked around the plant to see if I could locate the general foreman. We ran into one of the foremen, and the look on his face was unbelievable. He had a look that was total surprise, and at the same time, it was relief. I asked him where the general foreman was, and he said to me, "Where he always is," and pointed to a pickup truck near the work site with the headlights on.

The foreman asked if I wanted him to reach the general foreman by radio, and I said, "You know, I think I'll just walk over there myself." Still not sure who was at fault here or whom I could trust, I asked Jay to stay back with the foreman to make sure no radios were used.

As I was walking up to the driver's side window of the pickup truck, I realized the general foreman was not getting out or even looking at me. As I approached even closer, I could see he was sleeping at the wheel with the pickup truck motor off and the headlights on.

I knocked on the window, and the general foreman angrily awakened, and not knowing who he was even yelling at, he screamed, "What are you doing?"

I asked him to roll down the window, and he did about halfway. He realized it was me and said, "What are you doing here?"

I said, "Relieving you." I told him I was taking over the project from here on out. I told him he was to go to his hotel, pack his bags, and leave. "I'll need your room, and you are to report back to our supervisors at the corporate office first thing in the morning. By then I should have a full report for them as to your involvement with this project." He was later terminated.

I asked for Jay to gather up the four foremen so we could have a meeting. I wanted to get everyone's opinion as to where we were on this project and explain why we were there. Once we got that information ironed out, we could focus on the plan to correct the problems.

We were approaching 10:00 PM at this point, and I was concerned we were losing another day on the project. I wanted to make the meeting brief so we could get back to work, but that did not turn out to be the case. Once I started asking questions about the problems on the project, the foremen all explained to me how they all at one time or another talked to the general foreman about making better changes. They said they were just not being heard. I asked why they didn't call the corporate office and let someone know what was going on. They explained the general foreman had them convinced that they would be fired if they did not do what he said. They also said he told them he was in communication with the office but that the office only listened to his views as to what was going on. When the corporate supervisors came down for weekly meetings, they would walk the site with the general foreman, and some of the foremen explained their view of the problems, only to be ignored.

That made sense to me because my supervisors knew this project was a problem. They just wanted to ignore the fact that change was needed. They were hoping it would just work itself out, until the problem was out of control and I was called in to fix it.

The project was two very tall towers that we were working on. I split Jay and myself up. Jay was going to take the two best foremen, and I would take the other two, who were not that bad, just a little inexperienced. With the good plan the foremen, Jay, and I put together, I thought we would get the project back on track. I also figured the inexperienced foremen could learn from this mess, and I wanted to teach them through it.

Jay and I never left the project from the night we showed up with the clothes on our backs until it was finished. We picked up toothbrushes and other incidentals at a local convenience store, and we were fine.

The project finished two days ahead of schedule, and we all received a letter of appreciation from PG&E. The project was turned around, and the foremen bought into the changes because they were part of the changes, and they, just like Jay and me, wanted to do what was best for the company. We did not cheat on safety. We implemented more and better safety programs on the project. We not only brought in the project ahead of time, we reestablished the company name with PG&E. We stayed committed to safety, and we trained a couple of foremen. Most of these foremen came over with my partners and me to Bayview Environmental and are still with us today.

I think by getting everyone involved, you have a better chance of success than you would by going it alone. If you're a general foreman, foreman, principal, athletic director, or head coach, you know you can't do it alone anyway. You need help, and you need support. Don't be foolish and listen to just any single person. Listen to anyone who cares enough to talk to you about their ideas; you may not use the idea but you have someone interested in thinking and offering ideas and their experience. Listen to anyone who may have a need for your program to work. Listen, evaluate, and make the best decision for everyone.

If you hear from two of the four foremen working on one of your projects that they had some concern with the general foreman's decision making and you just ignore it, then you are being irresponsible and foolish. If you are a high school principal and you hear from five or six parents that they have issues with your head coach and you choose to ignore them, you are being irresponsible and foolish. I'm not saying these foremen or the parents are right, either. I'm just letting you know you're not doing your job if you ignore them.

Keep the open-door policy, and keep everyone in check. That's your job, and that is how you will remain on top of everything that is going on in your business and your programs.

12

Repeat It Constantly

One of the things I enjoyed the most about coaching was the fundamental drills. These drills are readily available at bookstores and online. I would develop some of the drills myself based on what I saw during a game or a mishap at practice. In some cases, you can view a tape or two and combine them to create a drill that would better suit your players.

I developed some fumble drills that were very successful with my players at the high school level. I wanted to have as many drills ready to go as I could. This would help keep practice fun and educational, no matter what position I was coaching. I felt it was my job to keep the kids' minds occupied while they were learning. Running the same drills day after day is just boring. Most of the drills I used were simulation drills (imitation or reenactment of an actual play or situation).

As a running backs coach, you need to work every day on things like ball-handling drills, balance drills, and fumbling drills. Along with these daily drills, you should add in a couple of other drills that are fun and focus on specific areas that need improvement. Make them different as well as educational. Along with your needed daily drills, add in a couple of other drills to take the boredom out of practice, like some blocking drills, sideline drills, reaction drills, passing drills, and bag drills. By mixing up practice drills and by keeping practice entertaining, you'll see a better turnout every day. You'll see your players getting better, and you'll see them more interested in learning. By having an organized practice with plenty of usable drills, you'll gain the respect from your players as well. Your players will see you as an organized, knowledgeable coach as opposed to a coach who is just getting through the day by winging the practice.

Have your area set up and ready to go. Don't wait for the players to set the cones or get the blocking bags out of the shed for you. It's their time to learn the drills, so don't waste it on them setting up the equipment. I would always get to practice a little early. This allowed me to get my areas set up. If things ran a little long, I would still have time to finish while the kids were doing team stretching.

As I mentioned above, one of the great things about coaching a sport today is the long list of tapes or books you can purchase online or at a bookstore. There is just no reason for any coach to come to practice unprepared. Once you understand your players' needs or you feel you could use some help coaching in a particular area that you are not comfortable teaching, buy a tape that focuses on the areas you want to work on.

If you need to work on blocking, receiving, reaction, balance, bag drills, cone drills, or ladder drills, they have them, and they are endless. You could pick drills from your favorite college or from your favorite coach. I prefer to select from a need such as poor pass blocking or punt return coverage and find a tape that will help.

In one of my fumble drills, I used a combination of some drills I got off of two tapes that I ordered from Championshipproductions. com. The first one was *Nebraska Football Series: Running Backs Drills and Fundamentals*, demonstrated by Nebraska's running backs coach. Another tape was *Quarterbacks and Running Backs*, made by an assistant coach from Iowa State (tape ID numbers are FV-1306D and FV-416, respectively).

I liked the "pull rip drill" for ball-handling control explained by the Iowa State coach, but for my kids, I preferred the ball position drill from the coach from Nebraska. In other words, I liked some things from both schools but preferred a mixture of both for my kids.

Taking some things from both of them made my team better. I felt that this was important, with the youth kids not being as strong as college players, so I took a little from both to make it work for my kids. Youth kids could hold the ball tighter at the chest plate and give less resistance when the arm was being pulled in an attempt to strip the ball or pull the arm away from the body.

In high school, we had weight training, and we implemented a program to help develop the running backs' biceps and forearms. At the high school level, I had the running backs press and hold the ball chest high through the linebacker level and then they could move the ball and press it to the ribs for better running, as described by the Iowa State coach.

The point here is both coaches' instructions are great. I used their experiences and coaching styles to help my program even though I had to alter their drills a little. The Iowa State coach used two players in his drills. For the high school kids, I use four. There is the ball carrier, of course, a player holding his jersey from behind, one on the left punching upward on the ball, and the fourth is on the right trying to pull the ball carrier's arm away from his body.

At the whistle, the ball carrier starts running with the ball in one hand pressed to his chest, and the other players start doing their duties. The player in the back is giving the runner some resistance by pulling the back of the jersey, and the players on the left and the right start punching and pulling. This drill will continue for five yards, the players release the runner, and the runner will continue running for an additional five yards. Then the players rotate positions and start all over. Be sure not to give too much resistance in this drill. It is not designed to slow the runner down, just give the runner some resistance. This also applies to the pullers and punchers. They are not at full speed either. They are just making an effort to remove the ball. You don't want to do this so hard it knocks over the runner. Focus on your drills. Mix them up for fun, and repeat your points constantly. Whatever position you are coaching, you need to repeat your key points, and you need to do it often. Keep reminding your players of the important points you are trying to teach, and when they tell you, "I know, Coach. I got it," remind them again.

Another reason I like the ball held up tight to the chest by my running backs is that it is hard for a defender to punch the ball out from behind. When our team was running scrimmages, I would stand five yards behind the running back and watch to see how they were carrying the ball. I could tell from behind the runner if it was being carried correctly or not from that point of view. If the football was being carried incorrectly, I'd see it from behind. It's right there under the runner's arm. If it was being carried correctly, I would not be able to see the ball at all. Every single play I would say to the runner, "Good carry," or "I saw the ball. Get it high and tight."

Your job as a coach is not over after the drill session is over. You have to drive home your points, you have to repeat your comments, and you need to do it constantly.

I would have the other running backs standing right next to me at five yards behind the runner. I could explain to the runners waiting to go in what I was looking for when they carried the ball. This way they would be learning while I was teaching another player. I would get them involved by telling the players next to me to watch a couple of plays. I would say to them, "Could you guys keep an eye on the runners and let them know if it was a good carry or not?" This was my way of getting them all involved and keeping them interested in the practice session. I was also teaching more than one player at a time. Once the runners knew their peers were watching, it became a bit of a game. They wanted to get it right the first time when they ran the ball, and they became very tough critics when someone else ran the ball. While they were being tough on each other, my points were being repeated constantly, and the kids were getting better and having a lot of fun doing it.

I do believe that having good drills and repeating my teaching points as often as I did contributed to why my running backs rarely fumbled. They averaged fewer than two fumbles a season, by my unofficial record, over a ten-year period. It did not matter who was carrying the ball, first-string or third-string. The fumbling drills and coaching points went to them all, and I had nothing but confidence with whoever's name was called to carry it.

During the games, it was the same thing: Focus on your players, get the best spot you can to watch their moves, watch the ball handling, and talk to your players when they come off the field. Repeat your points, and do it constantly. This is not the time to coach them up on their technique. No, this is the time to keep them focused on the points you have taught them.

As a coach, you can't start thinking your coaching duties are over just because it is game day. On game days, you need to go out on the field and coach up your players through warm-ups. Then you need to get alone with your players and repeat your coaching points from the week's practice.

Once your players return to the team, you calm yourself to being an observant coach.

I don't mean now it's time for you to watch the football game from the sidelines. You don't become an observer of the game. You need to be observing your players. This is not the time to tell the receivers coach that one of his receivers just ran the wrong route. That's not your concern. You need to be watching the running backs, if that is your job. If you're not the receivers coach, why are you watching his players? Work with the running backs and keep them focused on your points by repeating them over and over. During the game, remind your players that one fumble could dramatically change the outcome of the game. Keep them focused on your points. During the game, continue to coach up your players. Let them know you're watching and grading them.

When giving your players advice or giving them coaching points, make sure to get the backup players involved. They need to hear the same message. They may be in next, and you'll want them to be ready as well.

If one of your players makes a mistake during the game, reassure them it's going to be okay. They have to believe you have a plan for that too. If they see you calm and ready for a problem, they will shake the problem off much faster. You don't want to panic and start screaming at them. These are young kids, and that can be a little dramatic. So don't let them divert the problem into disappointment. If they hang their heads and start getting upset, you'll be spending too much time consulting this player instead of coaching the five or six other players on the field.

Let them know it's totally fine for now because you have a plan to right the ship. Take a mental note of the problem, and implement a drill for it tomorrow. You can get caught up on the entire game tomorrow while reviewing film.

Safety is what we repeat constantly at Demo Masters and Bayview Environmental. We have many reasons to keep our workers safe. First and foremost is the safety of our workers. Nobody wants to see an employee get injured. We understand our employees have families and people who depend on them, as we all do. Our employees are our friends as well. Most of our employees have been with us for well over ten years. They are people we care a great deal about, and we want them safe. Second, by keeping your employees safe and by lowering the number of injuries your company has, you'll save a lot of money on your workers' compensation insurance. Third, you will be able to record a lower mod-rate (this is a rating system; less than 1 is acceptable. For example, .83 is good). With a lower mod-rate you'll have more opportunities to work with the larger and more established companies. The better general contractors won't qualify subcontractors to do work for them if they don't practice safe work practices. The general contractors will measure your safe working practices by reviewing your health and safety plan along with your mod-rate.

Demo Masters' superintendents and I meet every Thursday after our sales meetings. We have discussions about our foremen and their needs, and we discuss every project in great detail. Then the superintendents get to sit there and listen to my repeated messages: "Make sure you guys are approving overtime before the crews work it. Make sure you guys are checking foremen and laborers to see if they are wearing their protective gear, safety glasses, hard hats, work boots, gloves, safety vest, ear protection, and anything else they may need in regards to the specific jobs requirements. Make sure we have only the amount of laborers we need on the job. Cut them back if someone is standing around, and get them more if they need them. Make sure you guys are going by and meeting with the general contractor's superintendent. I want him to know that you were there on the job and organizing our crews, discussing how they feel about our work, and what we can do better. Make sure you guys are reporting to the Demo Masters' project estimator on a daily basis. I want you to keep them up to date on their projects, and don't be afraid to get them involved if you need them. Make sure you guys get all work orders signed by the project superintendent before we start any additional work. Make sure you guys are making sure the foremen are repeating constantly our message to the laborers." That's right. They go out to the foreman, the foreman goes to the laborers, and we keep repeating our message constantly.

When you spend your time working on a business plan, and that business plan, through many years of trial and error, has finally reached a level that you could call nearly perfect, then why not repeat it constantly? Don't let your plan fall to the wayside because someone forgot the message or someone felt it has been said enough and people are tired of hearing it. If your company has a good, safe plan in place and you believe in the plan, then make sure you pass the plan on to everyone who is involved in it. Make sure the people below you pass the plan on down, just as you sent it to them. If you don't repeat it, then they will forget it or feel it is not that important. If you are the one who repeats it constantly, it will stick. If your employees see that you are being passionate about it, then they will get passionate about it, and they will understand that it is that important. Your employees will believe as you do.

If you're not repeating it, then the employees will not put the effort into the plan, the effort that the plan needs to survive. Without you repeating the plan, the plan will not last more than a week or two, and you'll be right back where you started. It's difficult to get people to change, but with a good plan to better the company, they will follow along. But who will they follow if not you? They need a clear, repeated message. Everyone must sell the message from the top down. That's the only way that your company's message will take on a life of its own. Once the word gets out that the company is making some positives changes, the employees will become interested and will want to be a part of the plan.

If the company is known by your employees as one for implementing change without some kind of follow-up or enforcement, then it will require even more of your efforts to reach them. You cannot start something new and two weeks later not enforce it and then decide to implement another program. Your inconsistency will create more confusion with the employees. They won't know if this is the real plan or if the real plan is coming next week. They will question their leaders about change instead of embracing it. They will question whether to go with this plan or wait for the one that may be coming next week. Who could blame them?

Get with the heads of your company and explain the plan to them, the importance of the plan, and get their input. Once the plan is finalized and everyone signs off on the plan, you need to explain in great detail how the plan will be presented to the employees. Then get the same message out to the employees and repeat it constantly.

The same thing applies to raising kids. You often tell them not to smoke. You know they might be out there smoking anyway with their friends, but you say it constantly every time they leave the house. Why do you think that is? Because you know that if your message did not set in this time, it might the next.

When your son or daughter asks you for the car keys, you recite the entire drivers education handbook. Why do you think that is? Because you know if you say it enough times, your child may be a little safer behind the wheel the next time they get the chance to drive. Sooner or later, it will stick.

You as a parent believe in those messages. You believe so much that you're willing to say it as often as you can. You don't care how much they say, "I know, Mom. Stop saying that. I know already." You don't care because you care about them and you believe in the message. Because of your experience in driving a car or your knowledge of what cigarettes can do to your health, you know you have a great message to tell your child. No matter how many times you have to repeat it, you're going to repeat it. Repeating a message constantly is a must for anyone who knows his or her message will help. When you know it's safer or you know it will make things work better, don't be afraid to keep repeating your message constantly. If your message is a good one and a successful one, then only a fool would not listen to it. So I guess you should repeat it again to them.

There is nothing different when building a message for the workplace or pushing your message with coaching points. When you have the right message, isn't it worth repeating constantly?

13

Guidance Through Football

I was in the fifth grade and my brother Kevin was in the sixth grade when we moved to the Pinole area. We were coming from a rough part of San Pablo, California. Our mother was always supportive of her four kids. The oldest is my sister Lori, then my brother Kevin, followed by myself, and our little sister Kelli.

My mom, who was pretty much a single mom most of our childhood, was always putting her kids first. As good as she was for my sisters and as hard as she tried with Kevin and me, she was not a dad. She was not a male role model at all. Of course, she taught Kevin and me how to be good people, and she taught us how to treat our elders with care and respect; however, she was not a dad.

We had a dad, Donald William Howell Sr., but he chose to leave his kids and wife for some other woman. He left our lives when I was three. I only saw him one other time before he died. It was at one of my football games during my senior year in high school. I remember looking up in the stands at the normal spot my mom, my brother, and my two sisters would sit. This particular time, my mom had a guest sitting with her, a strange-looking guy who kind of reminded me of Captain Kangaroo from that afternoon TV show. It was hard to see for sure because my mom sat high in the stands in our fairly large stadium. It was halftime, and the team and I headed back to the locker room through the stadium side gates, as we always did during home games. Mom had never met me there before, not in the four years I played football at the school. She met me there that day.

She said to me, "There is someone in the stands who would like to meet you."

I said, "Is it my dad?"

And she said, "Yes, how did you know?"

I told her, "Tell him it's too late, and I don't need him now. He can go back to where he came from."

She said, "I understand. You don't have to see him if you don't want to. I'll take care of it."

He died later that year from a heart attack, and I never got another chance to speak to him. That was a burden I carried for some time. Even through my twenties, certain things would remind me of that day that I acted like a kid who didn't need anybody, a kid who could show his dad that he made it just fine without him, even though I really wanted my dad to push everyone aside and say, "Let me go and talk to Donnie. I know what to say." But he didn't do anything.

It wasn't until I started coaching football and helping kids with their problems that I actually fixed my own. I often mentored kids about their parents; sometimes, their parents may seem to be hard on them, but what they did not know was their parents were really teaching them life's lessons. Their parents were teaching them from the mistakes they made in order to protect them from creating the same ones.

Through coaching football and helping the kids that I did, I realized it wasn't my burden to carry anymore. I was the child in that situation, and I needed him to act like the adult, a father, a mentor, and a friend, just like I always do for my kids and just like I did for the kids I coached. I spent more time with people I had never met and their kids than my dad ever spent with me. Sure, I probably wanted him to run down from the bleachers and scream out, "Son, I'm sorry I made a big mistake. Please let me talk to you for a while," but that didn't happen either.

I thought about it all the time. What if I had said, "Okay," when he wanted me to talk to him? What if I did not act like I was mad? Maybe I should have been nicer. It is sad for a young person to carry that kind of burden for as long as I did. But the truth is he was the adult and he should have demanded to see me. He should have told me that he and I needed to talk. He should have acted like an adult for once in his life. God knows I would have demanded to see my kids no matter what was in my way. Then again, I would never have left them either. That is something I'll never understand, leaving your own children behind, never calling to check in on them, never being curious enough to wonder what they were doing. How could you go about your day playing golf, mowing the lawn, celebrating at a party, and not giving a single thought to the fact that you have kids somewhere who can't eat tonight? That is just a crime for a person to be that selfish and thoughtless.

Here is a kicker for you. About ten years after my father passed away, my wife was looking into where my father was actually buried. Leslie found the place where he rests, and the cemetery told her during the conversation that his burial bill was never paid off. They told her he never received his nameplate because of an outstanding debt that was still owed. They told her he would not get his nameplate if the bill wasn't paid in full. Leslie and I covered the bill so my dad, who left my siblings and me behind, could have his nameplate. My father left behind brothers and sisters and even his mother at the time, and not one of them would pony up for the bill to put to rest their brother and son. Maybe they did not know?

It took a heartbroken son to put what had been done behind him and see to it that his father would not go without.

I think it is really hard for a single parent, especially a single mom with boys, to get them to stay focused in school and help them learn how to cope with issues without using anger. If boys and girls don't have a sport to play, they end up bottling up their tension. They don't understand how to release it. They end up showing bad behavior or uncontrolled behavior when they do try and release it.

Prior to moving from San Pablo to Pinole, my brother and I wanted as badly as anyone to play baseball. Early one spring morning, Kevin and I had a chance. One of Kevin's friends was trying out for a Little League baseball team, and he asked us if we wanted to go watch his tryouts. We didn't even know about tryouts but said we would.

Once Kevin and I got to the Little League park, we went to the bleachers and sat down to watch. Kevin and I soon became tired of sitting there and went down to the field. The Little League coach asked us if we wanted to try out. We explained to the coach that we had not signed up to play. He told us not to worry about it because there were a couple of days left for sign-ups and we should go home and ask our mom if we could sign up. I will never forget Kevin and I running home as fast as we could.

I was always a step or two faster than Kevin, which turned out to be a disadvantage in this case. As I reached for the front door handle of our apartment, Kevin was cutting into my lead with only a step to go. As I made a half turn on the door handle, Kevin was on me. We slammed into the door just as I opened it. The force of Kevin and my momentum put us on the living room floor, looking up at Mom. As we were looking up at Mom, we said in harmony, "Mom, can we sign up for baseball?" She said in a disappointed voice, "I'm sorry, kids. We can't afford it. I'm doing all I can for you four kids as it is. Maybe next year."

Next year never came. Neither my brother nor I ever played Little League baseball. That was tough for Kevin and me, but we did understand. I wondered at the time what I was thinking to ask for something like that in the first place. We knew what the answer would be, but we were young and got lost in the moment.

As we became older and as there were no sports for us to play, Kevin and I did the next best thing. We started fighting. Not each other, we fought any kid at any time we could. He and I were both pretty good at it, or I think we would have taken up fishing or something else like that. We fought all the time and actually liked doing it. We got out some aggression, and we got plenty of attention because of it.

We had no idea we needed sports, but we sure did. If we were not getting suspended from school, we were being held after school all the time. Luckily, some change came into our lives. A few years later, our mom remarried and we moved to a nice little subdivision called Bayview, near Pinole.

Kevin and I had to take a bus to our new school, Tara Hill Elementary School. I remember Kevin and I waiting all excited about meeting new people (well, at least I was). Kevin would let me meet people first, and then he would be happy to meet them a little later. We were sporting our best pompadour hairdos, and we had on our brand-new bell-bottom polyester slacks, not to be outdone by our big-collared silk shirts. We were ready to meet the new ladies on the bus.

The bus pulled up, and the giant double door slid open. Kevin and I got on the bus and started walking down the long, narrow aisle. It did not take us long to see that we might be overdressed. This bus was loaded with country bumpkins. The kids were really hard on Kevin and me that first day to and from school. We knew we would have problems for some time. Some of the bigger kids on the bus, who thought they were tougher than us, were making jokes about our hair, our clothes, and whatever else they could think of. On our way back home, as we were getting close to our stop, one kid was about two inches from Kevin's face getting brave and making his jokes. The bus stopped, and Kevin and I got off the bus and listened to their laughter as we walked away. Kevin did not say much the rest of that day.

The next morning was pretty much the same thing. We got to the bus stop and waited for the bus. When the bus made the turn and started down the hill to our stop, Kevin looked at me and said, "Nobody is going to pick on us today; are you with me?"

I replied, "Hell yeah."

Kevin got on the bus first, and I followed. As we walked down the narrow aisle, I could see about four rows ahead of Kevin as he was walking toward the kid who was having the most fun at our expense from the day before. The kid yelled out for everyone to hear, "Looker here, the pompa-duper hairdo guys are coming." Kevin just kept walking until he reached the brave kid and punched him square in the face about five enormous times. A couple of his buddies tried to help him, but I took care of that. We kicked the crap out of the kids on that bus that day.

That was all we knew; if you get challenged, then you step it up a little. It was just not our way back then to run from a fight. These poor country kids must have thought if they picked on us enough, we would cry or run away or something. Boy, were they wrong.

It wasn't long before we gave in and got a little country ourselves. The next year, my brother went on to middle school (seventh and eighth grades) and I went to the brand-new elementary school that was built in our little town of Bayview. That's when I discovered football. The school was called Seaview. All the classrooms were named after flagships or something like that. The school had an after-school program that had football, and I wanted to play. It was free, and I had to spend a good portion of my time after school anyway for being punished, so why not play football instead?

In our area, there were about six or seven grammar schools, so the after-school league was pretty big and pretty competitive, for flag football, that is. There were only two youth football teams in the area, and you had to be twelve to fourteen years old to play. There were two middle schools and only two high schools in the area as well. Most of the kids you played with in the after-school league would end up as teammates or you would be playing against each other later in youth or high school football. Everyone knew everyone.

Our team the first season at Seaview was not loaded with talent, but we had fun and competed. At the time, I was one of the few Seaview kids who would shine on the football field. Most of the kids who lived in the Bayview development were not as troubled as I was. They were playing football for fun. I was playing for attention.

In our first two games, I started the game by returning the opening kickoffs back for touchdowns. Soon this became pretty regular. I was returning kickoffs back a lot. Not always the opener, but during the game at some point, I would return a kickoff.

Like most of the grammar school flag football teams, we had cheerleaders. Our cheerleading squad started a chant that went, "Go Donnie Go, Go Donnie Go, Go, Go, Go Donnie Go," which I thought was really neat. However, many years later my high school football teammates told me once they heard that chant, they wanted to kill me. They told me they would say, "Who is this Donnie guy? And why does he have his own cheerleading squad?" We laugh about it now, but it was something that I needed very much back then. I felt the game of football was bringing me to a place I liked very much. It was a place that I did not want to mess up. I felt important and needed.

During school, I was a clown. Being a class clown would get me recognized, and by being the funny guy, no one would notice that I was hiding the fact that I could not spell, and by being the funny guy, they may not notice the fact that I was terrible at reading. I definitely did not want anyone to notice that I was an average or below-average student. Today, I'm still a clown, but that's because I just like seeing people happy.

I was good at flag football, and I wanted to keep playing. I even made good grades during football season so my mom wouldn't take it away. I used football to get my fix for attention. It was all I had.

When I turned twelve years old, I signed up for youth football with the Pinole Junior Spartans. After a few weeks, I was going up against the fourteen-year-olds. I was very small in size but could hit like a truck. I loved the contact of the game. Bring it as hard as you can, and it will hurt less. That was my way of thinking, and it's true. Hit the other player as hard as you can, under control of course, without hesitation, and I promise, the person who resisted will take the brunt of the hit.

By the time I was in high school, I was still fighting some; my grades were fine as long as I was playing football. As soon as football season was over, my grades went in the tank.

Even though I never really took my football career anywhere, I still believe that football made me a better businessperson than I would have been without it. Football was a tool that guided me through some tough times as a kid, like coming home to a house that had no electricity because the utility company had to shut it off from lack of funding from my stepfather, or the landlord stopping by threatening to evict us. The last thing a small kid needs to worry about is moving again. Our mom was constantly trying to cover up the bad news, but we always knew what was really going on. Troubled kids need to have an activity to let their minds focus on something other than adult-type problems.

It's a tough world out there, and we all understand that, but can't you find a way as a coach to put a little joy into a troubled kid's life? You know who they are. They can't hide their burden like adults can. Football gave me the skills to compete. It introduced me to some great people, and it gave me the ability to challenge myself. Football introduced me to friends, coaches, parents, and kids I will know and respect for years and years.

Without being introduced to football or having my life guided by football, I don't think I would have ever created some of the successes that I was blessed to have made. Football gave me a way to help troubled kids and that is as rewarding for me as it might be for them. I may have ended up in some kind of prison if not for football. Some of the people my brother and I knew ended up there. It's no joke. Football can change lives. So I hope you remember that the next time you're coaching a kid or giving one of your child's friends a ride to practice. They too may be playing for something more than football.

It was easy for me to think of myself as an underachiever after high school; my football was all but over. The short stay I had at San Francisco State was a joke, and I already told you about my spelling and reading. I was not illiterate or anything like that, but I sure wish they had a spelling checker on typewriters back then. I was a hardworking kid though and that's something I always told my sons: always be a hard worker and good things will come your way. I have worked as long as I could remember, as far back as when I was selling the candy from the guy in the parking lot. I would do whatever I could to make some money. Mow lawns, paint fences, dig a ditch, pull weeds, or whatever needed doing. I was ready. I worked hard enough to get return business as well. Nobody or no company ever let me go. I could not imagine a company firing me. I don't know what I would have done if an employer came to me and said, "I think we are better off here at Brand X Company without you." I would just crawl under a rock in disbelief. How could they be better off without me? I work too hard for that to ever happen.

I got my first real job when I was a senior in high school, working at Mercury Dry Cleaners, taking in and tagging clothes. I worked the drive-through and collected people's clothes from their car windows. They would hand them to me, and I would tag them and place the clothes in the laundry bins. That job was pretty good paying for a high school kid, and it was fun too.

I learned a pretty good lesson from one of the owners of Mercury Dry Cleaners. This guy was right from Rough Town, USA. He was born and raised in Chicago and tough as nails. He had the old, scratchy voice to go with it. On my first day there, he asked me to follow him to the back of the shop, and I did. He showed me the back perimeter brick wall, which had a steel exterior door and a large black fan above it. The fan was built into the wall. The fan would suck the hot air from the shop and exhaust it outside.

He pointed with his large, fat, slightly bent index finger at the black fan and said, "The fan used to be shiny." The fan was definitely not shiny now, and we could both see that. He said, "Tiger, go get the ladder and remove the shroud from the fan and clean it. I'll be back soon."

I was on the job. I got the ladder as directed, removed the shroud, cleaned the fan, replaced the shroud, put back the ladder and cleaning products, and gave my work the once-over. It was shiny now. I went and got the owner, and he said, "Where is my ladder?"

I said, "I put it back. We can see the fan from here."

He said, "Go get the ladder, Tiger, and take off the shroud. I need to inspect the fan."

I said, "Okay," and did as he asked. He stuck his head into the fan as if it was the first time he had seen one and said, "It's not waxed. You did not wax the fan."

"No, I didn't. You said for me to clean it, and I cleaned it, and it's shiny," I replied.

He told me to repeat everything I had already done and this time wax it too. I repeated everything as he said, and I asked him to come and see it, this time leaving everything off and putting away nothing. He climbed the ladder and stuck his head deeper into the fan than before and swiped the fan with his large, fat, slightly bent index finger and said, "Feels like one coat of wax. Start over from the beginning and give it two coats of wax." Again, I repeated the steps and gave the fan its second coat. I went to find the owner and asked him to come back for another look. He climbed the ladder and stuck his head into the fan and pointed with his fat hobbler's index finger and said, "It's just not working. I think you should strip off the wax and repaint the fan."

I lost it at that point. I said very loudly to him, "You have to be the biggest idiot I have ever met. It's amazing you can wipe your own butt. I quit."

I left the building and walked, seriously, about seven miles home. When I got home, my stepfather was on the phone, laughing his butt off. He said the phone was for me. It was my former boss. He said, "Hey, Tiger, you did well. I'll see you tomorrow."

"What the hell are you talking about?" I asked.

He told me he always tested his employees out on the first day. He said he only wanted someone with moxie to work for him. "If you have moxie, I'll trust you because you stand up for what is right," he said. "I like to see how far I can push someone before they quit, and you did well, although nobody ever asked if I can wipe my own butt before. See you tomorrow."

I had a lot of good times at Mercury Dry Cleaners. As for the owner, he just liked being around people like him.

I traded that job a couple of years later for an opportunity to work as a machinist, making stainless steel parts for the medical and industrial industry. While I was still a machinist, I married Leslie in May of 1981, and then around 1984, I wanted to do something else. I was getting tired of the machinist thing and really preferred to be working outside. I discussed it with Leslie, and she said, "Go ahead and figure out what will make you happier."

I was good at doing my own landscaping, building decks and fences, installing lawns and sprinklers, and other things that pertain to landscaping. I thought I would start doing landscaping on the side. I started doing a few jobs for my friends and family, and it was going pretty well until one customer asked me if I had a license. A license? I did not know I would need a license to do landscaping. My mind started to melt down just knowing I would have to take a test. There was no way I could pass a test to be a contractor. "I'm just a dummy from San Pablo," I would tell myself. I stayed a machinist. I didn't even try to get a license. I knew I was stupid. Why try?

Later I had the opportunity to move on and start a new career in the environmental business. When I wasn't working at the environmental shop, I was working with some friends who were general contractors. I loved doing this kind of work. It was outside, and every couple of weeks you could go and work someplace new and meet some new people. It was really fun stuff. I decided to get my general contractors license (B), then I would get my asbestos license (ASB), I would start my own company, and life would be great.

Not so fast. I forgot I was terrible at reading and spelling. I signed up for the test and received a test date. The test was in about six weeks, so I needed to study. I went to a contractor's bookstore in Berkeley, California, and bought the appropriate books. I spent three to four weeks reading those mind-numbing books. I spent more time on the law portion of the book because I knew everything about the trade. My time was better spent on the law.

I was set up for the exams with the law in the morning and the trade in the afternoon. I needed every bit of the two hours I got for the law exam, and it was worth it. The good news came that I had passed the law exam. Time for the cakewalk trade exam. Well, I don't think I could have bombed any worse than I did that afternoon. I didn't have a clue as to what the exam was looking for, and I failed. I was so disappointed with myself. I was just depressed and mad all at the same time. How could I blow this opportunity? What was I thinking in the first place? I was never good at school, and I knew I was terrible at reading and spelling. Maybe I should just understand that I was going to be the really good working guy who works for someone else my whole life.

My wife said to me, "Just slow down and spend more time focusing on your plan. Keep studying, and keep trying." She also said, "When have you ever stopped trying for something you wanted?" She was right.

I went to a contractor's school and took some self-study night classes and aced the test the next time through. With the confidence I learned playing football and the support that came from my wife, I now have licenses in California and Nevada: B, C-21, ASB, and Hazardous Materials.

I was at a bookstore one day with Leslie, and I saw this book titled *Straight A's Never Made Anybody Rich*. I liked it mainly because of the title. The book was written by Wess Roberts, Ph.D. There is a paragraph in the book that reads, "If your child is just average, how can you compete? You've lost from the outset. Surely your average child will never amount to more than average as an adult. If your child is below average, there may be no hope at all. Right?" Wrong! Rest assured, this line of thinking is utter nonsense!

The book and this paragraph got me thinking about myself a little, mostly about being average. I was acting average, but I was never average at anything. My mind was always looking to do something else. I was never satisfied or complacent. The book also mentioned things like personal achievement, and I'm the kind of person who is always willing to take some thought-out chances. I started thinking about football and how much I learned about myself through it and how I worked hard at it because I was going to be good at it or would die trying.

I believe in personal achievements, and I believe in earning your way. That's when I said I would never consider myself stupid again. I would focus on what I wanted to do and make sure I wanted it and then work hard until I got it.

Football and the coaches I had taught me that you have to work hard for what you want. They taught me confidence. They taught me teamwork. And they taught me how and why you get and give respect.

Donnie Howell

The book *Straight A's Never Made Anybody Rich* sits on my bookshelf behind my desk at my corporate office in Oakland. I recommend it to teachers and coaches as a tool with insight because a lot of our work with kids is the same.

14

Respect Brings Respect

I think the biggest mistake a high school coach can make today is treating high school football players like kids. Talking down to a young adult is a huge mistake. They should not be talked at like they are little children. They are young men and women. You should direct your tone when talking to these young adults as if you were giving advice to one of your adult friends. Some of these young people are eighteen and vote, some may be fighting for our country in a war. They have developed opinions based on discussions with their mothers or fathers. Some need to hold jobs to help Mom or Dad at home. They have earned the right to be spoken to like a young adult. There are kids like I was who had to work over the summer just to buy next year's school clothes. Believe it or not, some of these kids have to help raise a disabled sibling with a crack-addict mother or father at home. These young men and women have problems just like you do. They have issues at school or at their jobs, and they may have problems with you, their coach, who might talk down to them. They have daily issues just like everybody else. The difference is they are young adults who don't know how to handle their problems as maturely as they should. I said "should" for a reason, because some older adults can't act maturely either.

You should know that these kids need you to talk to them as if they were adults. You will gain much more respect from these players if they feel you are treating them as adults and not as children.

I liked treating the kids as my equal. Most of the kids I coached respected me for it, plus they had some great jokes that we would share. I showed every kid who played for me respect. I would ask how their day was. I would ask them how yesterday's problem was going, if they shared one with me the day before. I would make it a point to ask about their families and their schoolwork. I would be honest with them about their role with the team if they asked, "Hey, Coach. Why am I not playing more?"

"Well, son," I would say, "I've asked you many times to work on your ball handling. You have caused too many fumbles in practice, and I'm not comfortable putting you in right now. Show me you will work harder at it. And if you are in control of the ball, I'll reconsider." Straight, honest, and truthful.

Would you like it if, when you asked your boss for some feedback, he gave you a line of crap? I didn't think so. Respect is a two-way street; you give it, and it comes back. Treat these young adults the way you want to be treated.

One hot summer day at Clayton Valley, I was coaching my running backs on the lower end of the field. The head coach blew the whistle for our fifteen-minute break. The team was broken up into individual groups, which were spread all over the field. Once the coach called for a break, all players met up together at the water stand for a cool drink. After they had their water, they would lie down in the shade for some relaxation.

About ten minutes later, I was walking by the players lying in the shade. These players were rolling around in hysterics. These guys were laughing and rolling in the grass like hyenas. I looked over and started laughing myself just because they were laughing so hard. I said, "Okay, guys. Let me in on it."

They said, "No, Coach, we can't tell you. We will get in big trouble."

I said, "How much trouble can a person get into if it is that funny?"

They said, "We will tell you if you promise not to tell." I agreed.

They explained to me that just as the linemen joined the others in the shade, the assistant's coach came over and told one of the players to run back to the weight room to get his hat and whistle that he, himself, had left behind. The player pleaded with the coach for him to get it himself. The player said he was tired from the heat and needed to rest. The coach yelled at the player to get the hat and whistle or he would make the player run in the heat for the duration of the practice. So, the player got up and ran the 300 yards back to the weight room and retrieved the coach's stuff.

I looked back over my shoulder and saw the assistant's coach from a distance blowing his whistle for the kids to end their break.

I said, "Okay, boys. That's enough. Before break time is over, what was so funny?" The players said he went and got the coach's whistle and hat for him as he asked, but when he got into the weight room, he grabbed the hat and whistle and rubbed them all over his private parts. This coach was blowing that whistle like there was no tomorrow.

Show respect to those young adults if you ever plan on them giving you any. This was a complete lack of respect by the coach and the player. Neither had respect for the other. This coach had no business asking a player on his break to run and get something he forgot. This was the players' time to relax. They didn't get much time for breaks as it was. This coach had no thought to the player's time. Instead, he thought this player would want to be his little servant and run something down for him in the heat. "Yes, Coach. I would love to chase down your stupid hat and whistle." Come on, Coach. What are you thinking?

This coach was a tool and a complete embarrassment to coaches everywhere. However, this player had so little respect for this coach that he would actually rub the coach's whistle on his private parts. This particular coach was always rude or mean to the players and because of it they felt no respect for him. To be honest, I did find it funny that this happened to him. But it really is a statement of respect. If the coach had respect for the player, he would have retrieved his own hat and whistle. And if the player had respect for the coach, he might have offered to go and get the hat and whistle for him. Be careful around these young adults, because just like you, they won't take much crap from someone they don't respect. Would you?

The coach who runs his group of players with intimidation and screaming is the coach who is running his group without respect. These types of coaches are the ones whose players will lose focus sooner. They are the ones bored with practice. This type of coach is sucking all the fun out of the reasons these kid are playing football in the first place. The coach will see the kids working hard and acting interested when he is nearby. They will act interested, but they won't work hard when the coach is not around. They won't work on the skill the coach may be trying to teach on their own or after practice simply because they lost interest in the coach, and they have no respect for him either. These coaches are fooling themselves into thinking they are doing good work. They are fooling themselves if they think they are reaching these young adults.

I remember once, during a night game, we were playing against a local rival. We were the visitors at this game, and I was on the sidelines watching my running backs. I could see from across the field the home team had the chain gang on their own sideline. This is normally on the visitor's sideline so the announcers while calling the game can see the yardage markers, plus it is distracting and a nuisance to the visitors. That's why, when you are the home team, you put it on the visitor's sideline. But this night was different. I was standing on our sideline, and I noticed a parent walking from the home team's sideline to the back end zone, the end zone in which we were about to score again. We were winning the game pretty handily and scored again in the end zone where the parent was standing. Our coach called for a one-point conversion, a kick through the uprights. However, our kids bobbled the snap, picked the ball up, and ran it in for a two-point conversion.

To some, it may have looked like we were going for the two points to run up the score, but that was not the case. Not with our coach. I saw the coach call for the one-point conversion, no doubt. I looked over and saw the parent from the end zone walking briskly toward me. He looked angry and was pushing up his sleeves as he was approaching me. I quickly got myself ready for what may happen. The parent started yelling at me before he came too close and said, "Are you the head coach?" He repeated, "Are you the head coach?"

I said, "No, I'm not."

He said, "I can't believe you guys would show our kids such little respect and try to run the score up like that."

I said, "You have it all wrong, buddy. It was a mistake on the snap. We did not try to go for two." He did not care. He just wanted to get at the head coach, and I was not letting him. If I did, there would have been some problems that could have been ugly for everyone. As he got closer, I started to notice something about this parent. He was drunk, and I started to smell it. I tried to explain to him what happened, and I asked him if he had been tilting a few that evening. He said that he indeed had two or three but that was no excuse for our team not showing his kids any respect.

I was starting to get irritated by this clown, so I asked him to leave. After we exchanged some words, I asked him to leave again. This time, I had him by the arm, walking him out. I asked him how he thought he was going to get us to respect his players when he did not even respect himself enough to stay home when he had been drinking that much. He said, "I'm sorry, but it's been a bad night." Maybe he had problems that I didn't know about, but one thing is for sure, I gave him no respect.

Respect is something most people think they are entitled to. I don't think most of them use the same definition of respect that I do.

You see, some of you think that you're entitled to respect simply because you are the head coach or the project superintendent or the owner of the company. Why exactly do you think you should get the respect? Because you are in charge? That's not good enough. Being in charge will get you the big job title or the cool parking space, and it may require the people who work for you to listen and follow, but they don't and they won't just give you respect. That has to be earned. I don't believe being promoted is a reason to think the position automatically comes with respect.

Well, the one exception is the president of the United States. They get respect with the job until they are in the office for a year, and then they lose it. With that being said, you are not the president of the United States.

I think you should expect respect from the people around you because you give respect to those who earn it. Humbling yourself to work hard for the program or the business is where you want to go. The people around you who can learn from your examples are the ones who over time will learn to trust you and appreciate your dedication and your passion to make the program or business work. They will give you the respect you deserve because you gave them the respect as they earned it right along with you.

You did not give them respect the first day you met them. You watched them, they developed, you learned to trust them, and you learned to respect them. Over time, some of them did not earn your respect the same way that you gave the others respect by observing them over time through their actions. That is my definition of respect, and it works with young adults, with coworkers, with assistant coaches, and with parents too.

Just about all of us have worked with a guy in our office who was never on time for a meeting, didn't have a positive opinion about anything, and refused to help if you did not vote his way. Then a couple of days later, you hear him in the break room telling the boss what an awesome job he did to save the project.

We have all been around the woman on our team who missed the evening meetings, returned important calls too late, and fell short of completing her portion of the project because she fell behind while talking to friends on the phone. Other team members jumped in and helped her complete the task. However, she was the first one at the presentation meeting, front and center, ready to gobble up the credit.

The same goes for bosses. They will give out assignments to people on their staff and pressure them to complete them in a timely fashion. Once they receive the report from you, it hardly gets read. Your boss walks it over to his boss and hands it over to him. Your boss gets some really nice compliments from his boss on the work. He never mentions the people who helped put it together. He just takes the credit and moves on.

Why would anyone give respect to any of these types of people? Why would anyone think they should be respected? The boss who always reminds you that you work for him, the boss who thinks you're there to get him coffee, the boss who throws his staff under the bus to make himself look better, the boss who demands perfection from you and can't find any for himself, and the boss who thinks you owe him respect because he is your boss. These are the people, the bosses, who just don't get it. Just like the coaches whose players are not working hard when he is not close by. The players lost respect, and that applies to business as well.

If you are operating without respect from your employees, I suggest you work on it fast. Your employees will work hard when they see you, and they will not give a damn when they don't. You need to have employees who work hard whether you are side by side with them or not. You are the manager of your people.

I've told you about our meetings at Demo Masters and Bayview Environmental in an earlier chapter. My partners and I always had an open dialog with our office employees. They too have an open-door policy just like the field staff and our superintendents. I think our business plan with our employees allows them to feel comfortable about speaking freely with us. They know we will implement their ideas or we will explain why their idea will not work this time.

This is respect. My partners and I are showing respect to our employees by giving them a strong voice in the company. If they feel strongly about helpful change, then we feel strongly about making the change. They are smart people, they are capable of running a company just like we can, and they prove it every day. So why on earth should we think they owe us respect? Well, we do have bigger offices.

I like the guys who say, "Boy, I sure respect my wife. After all, she has put up with me over the years, the drunken nights coming home, the fights, the money I lost, trouble with the law, and she is still with me after all these years." Well, that's not respect. That's thanking God. That's counting your blessings. That's being thankful. That's unbelievable. That's lucky that she did not leave you. And I'll tell you something else. You might have respected her if she did leave.

While you're thinking that you respect her for not leaving, do you think she respects you? Do you think she calls her girlfriends and tells them how much she respects the fact that you're not home again or that you are out probably losing more of the money that you two don't have or you are leaving now to go to one of your many court dates? I'm sure her girlfriends are envious and wishing they were in her shoes. I think she loves you, and you should give her real respect by slowing that behavior down and appreciating her part in the marriage. By you going first, she will follow your lead, and the two of you will truly have respect for each other through sacrifice and commitment.

I'm not claiming to be Mr. Neat Guy here. Leslie and I got married when she was nineteen years old and I was twenty, so we had our learning curves also. I'm just giving you my insight to a shortcut for respect. Respect her or lose her, I like to say.

Take the time to speak to your players as if they were no different than one of your adult friends. When speaking to one of your employees, speak to them as if they were one of your friends; ask yourself, Would I talk to my friends that way? By giving respect to your players, coworkers, employees, family members, and even your friends, you will find them wanting to learn more from you and listen more to what you have to say, and that, my friend, is them giving you respect.

15

The Good Times

The Pinole Valley Spartans opened the 1978 season with a record of four wins and no losses. It was the beginning of week five, and we were starting to get some attention from around the league. We were also getting noticed by the local radio station, KNBR, which came out to do an interview with some of our players. This was a big deal back then in our area. Pinole, California, was not like Texas, where local television covered their high school sports and you read about the local players in the newspaper. Around here nobody had ever before heard of a radio station coming to your school to interview your football team and talk to some of their players. The following week, we had a game scheduled with Moreau Catholic High School, which also had four wins and no losses to start their season.

Our head coach, Jerry Dueker, was a smart guy. He prepared the players to speak well and to minimize their emotions. He did not want his players acting disrespectfully. He did not want his players embarrassing the school or the community.

The radio personality started the interview with our star quarterback, Gary Torretta. They discussed a few minor issues and then moved on to our matchup against Moreau. The interviewer asked Gary what he thought our chances were against a powerhouse like Moreau. Gary replied, as he always did (and still does to this day), with a very well-thought-out answer. Gary said, "We will play as hard as anyone. I know our team, and I would not bet against us. Moreau has a great coach and a great program. We are looking for a great game."

That was very mature of Gary, I thought, and I was damn glad they didn't ask me that question. The interviewer moved on to ask questions of some of the other players, and for the most part, everyone was gracious and respectful to Moreau. After all, they were a pretty good football team, and we knew it.

The following day, after our radio interview, we read an interview in the newspaper from the Moreau Head Coach, who said that they had no fear of playing us. The paper portrayed the Moreau players as faster and tougher than we were. The paper mentioned from their view that the Moreau players were bigger and more dominant. They made statements about how our team was lucky to be undefeated and how we barely won the games we did. They made comments as to our schedule not being as tough as theirs. They said they would come into our home field (we were the home team that year) and leave still undefeated. Their coach made additional comments too, none of them very humbling.

We as players were really mad. We wanted to redo our radio interview. We were upset big time. Coach Dueker said to us in the locker room, "This is why I didn't want us to act overconfident. Look how mad you guys are right now. We have to settle our emotions down and focus on the game plan. We will show them how bad they messed up by getting the Spartans upset. I'm going to leave these newspaper articles on the wall in the locker room all week. This will be our focusing point." He did. Coach Dueker left the article up on the wall for us to look at all week. I can't speak for everyone, but I'll tell you it fired me up pretty well. Moreau went home that evening with their first loss. We pounded them 35 to 0.

I feel very fortunate that I somehow found this game (or it found me). Football has helped me grow in many ways. I have many friends today who I met through football, some I played with, and some I played against. The starting quarterback for our cross-town rival school, De Anza High, was Steve Tuite. Steve is one of my best friends today. Steve and I play as golf partners in our member/guest golf tournaments each year. My Oakhurst member/guest is in June, and Steve's, at Green Valley, is every July. Now I'm not chasing him around the offensive backfield anymore, looking for another sack, but we can still compete against each other for a few bucks on our monthly golf outings.

I find it kind of sad that more people don't have but a few friends that they can say they've been really close with. I know I'm lucky to have as many as I do, but it's not just luck, it's also staying in touch with the people you care about. They stay in touch with you and you stay in touch with them; it's a two-way street. All of us get busy at times, and it's easy to get into a routine of your own, but slow down and find a minute to send a friend a text message, give them a phone call, or send an e-mail; your friends will appreciate it and they will do the same. Be thankful you have the friends you do; a lot of people may only have two or three, which is even more reason to stay in touch with them.

I think that the game of football gave me something in common with the long-term friends I have today. I think we all realized that we are alike in many ways. We have surrounded ourselves with people who like to compete, people who enjoy football, and people who like golf, fishing, and family.

By starting with football, I was able to move into a better type of social group. I was able to break myself away from becoming the ordinary, drug-using and poverty-stricken kid. Because of football, the other players accepted me as one of their teammates, and from that, we also became friends; they did not care if I was rich or poor, they just gave me a chance to be one of them because we loved football. These kids came from families with better principles and upbringing than my family had. I was able to learn from their parents as they taught their children about things like politeness, respect, and a sense of values. If you're a younger person reading this book, trust me when I say, Find a sport you love and get mixed up in it right away. Keep an open mind and see where it takes you.

When I was growing up in San Pablo, before football came my way, I had a friend the same age as me and we would play outside after school, like tag and baseball, ride bikes, and stuff. We were about nine years old when both of our families moved away from that area. I did not know it at the time, but his family moved to El Sobrante, California, home of De Anza High School, and I moved to Pinole, home of Pinole Valley High School. We were in neighboring cities and our schools were big-time rivals.

When we were both twelve years old, I saw my little old friend for the first time since I was nine. He was playing for the El Sobrante Titans youth team, and I was playing for the Pinole Junior Spartans. Both teams were going through warm-ups on the field when he came over to me and said, "I think I know who you are; you are Donnie Howell, aren't you?" He then asked me if I remembered him. I said I did, of course. We talked and got caught up for a few minutes, and I noticed he was wearing the same number that I was. We discussed the numbers, and he asked me what position I was playing. I told him I was the starting running back and the starting linebacker. He replied he too was playing those same positions. Here it was, about three years later, and through football, we found each other again and had the same jersey number and played the same positions. We didn't get lost from each other again, although I don't see him as much anymore because he and his family now live in Southern California. Oh, by the way, he is a successful contractor like me also. People who have common interests will find each other. Football is a great way to get your life moving if you are a struggling kid, if you are having social problems, or if you're feeling lost. Get with your local youth football program and start meeting people. You may have a lifetime of not regretting it, like me.

You take tough skills you learned from playing football, and you take the skills you learned from being around people with great principles and ethics, and you become a coach. Coaching is almost as rewarding as playing the game of football. The number of people I have met through coaching is amazing, people who live in my community I never knew before or probably never would have met if not for coaching.

How would you know whether someone is like you or not if you don't speak to them? How do you ask a person you bumped into at the grocery store if they want to bring their spouse over for dinner? What do you say to this person? "We've seen each other three times at the grocery store, so you must be like me. Get your family, and let's meet for dinner." I don't think so!

My wife and I have met some really great people over the years from football. We have friends from coaching together. We have friends who are the parents of our kids' teammates, we have friends from sports vendors selling embroidery or uniforms, we have friends who are parents we met in the stands, and the list just goes on and on. Where else are you going to meet so many people and enjoy the same things for many years if it is not football or some kind of sport? Get involved. You won't believe what you will see and who you will meet.

Every couple of months, some of my high school football buddies and I meet for dinner. There are about six or eight of us, and it continues to grow. When one of us runs across an old friend or teammate, somewhere in the conversation the question will come up, "Have you seen so-and-so lately?" And the reply will be, "Yeah, I do. A bunch of us get together every couple of months and go to dinner. Why don't you come next time?" And they normally do. I thank God all the time for giving me a great wife, kids, friends, the smarts to rise, and the ability to love and respect others. And I'll even give up a shout from time to time for the path he chose for me through football.

There are good times at work too. You can have a great deal of fun at work. With the economy headed in the direction that it is going in today, I feel it's important for young adults to understand that this is what we really are. We are Americans who are known for our ability to work. We have always been about work. The good thing about the economy going bad is that it will remind us that nothing is free. We always worked hard for what we wanted, and we appreciated it more when we got it.

Our kids were losing that. In my unscientific opinion, I felt the kids of today were heading for a life of entitlement. Some of these adults are still considered kids by their parents at the age of thirty.

Kids? They are not kids. If you were thirty years old when I grew up, you were an adult. You did not call your mom or dad to help you with your bills. You did not need a place to live. Your dad was not out trying to find you a job because you were living at his house.

As the money became good for the middle class, the more they gave to their kids. I'm no exception. I did it too. But the one thing I always did was convince my kids that they should be good, hard workers. I wanted them to understand if they did not have me to rely on, they could rely on themselves.

If you are a teenager now and you are not sure where your life is heading and you don't have someone to lean on, then never forget this: Every employer in the USA wants and needs good, hardworking people.

Pride yourself in the fact that you will become the best employee that anyone has ever seen. Be on time and make that a priority. Be reliable. Be professional. Help wherever you can. Always stay busy when at work. If your assignment is completed and you can't find your supervisor, grab a broom and sweep or help a coworker with their duties until your supervisor comes back around. Don't just sit on your butt somewhere and wait for something to do. Make it your rule to only talk to your friends at home or on your break. Don't use your cell phone to talk to friends while at work. Be polite and respectful, and dress appropriately at work. You're not in a gang, so don't look like it.

I promise you will have a great life if you are considered a great employee. The cool thing about being a great employee is anybody can be one, and it doesn't matter if you are rich, poor, black, white, whatever. Anybody can do better for themselves. It might be hard to get the chance to prove to everyone that you can do it, but keep trying, and it will happen. You will get that first job, and you will show everyone else what they're missing.

Our kids will rebound too, just like us. The adjustment may be tough at first, but I'm sure most kids will realize they have the tools to work hard too. And once they find work, they will see how fun and rewarding it is. Once you realize that you don't need your mom and dad's money anymore or you find that you can make your own, it's a great feeling. You are really independent now. You have figured it all out now, and you have met some people who are your age, and they figured it out as well. Plus having your own money to party with is pretty cool too.

Okay. Wait a minute on that one for now. Before we have money to party with, we are going to follow a little rule for ourselves as well. We have become great workers, now let's become smart with our little bit of money.

Your paycheck comes in on Friday, and you put two thirds of it into your checking account and one third of it goes into your savings account.

If you know your total monthly bills, then you can budget your party money weekly.

For example: Say your total bills are $2,560 a month (rent, utilities, car payment, insurance, food, etc.) and your weekly paycheck (after taxes) is $1,240 a week; if you put one third of it into savings, it would be around $413. You would now have $827 in your checking account per week. $827 × four weeks is $3,308 to pay your bills at the end of the month. So we have $3,308 minus your monthly bills of $2,560, which will leave you with a balance of $748. Divide that by four weeks and now you know that you have $187 to party with every weekend. Now you're being responsible and having a little fun. Plus, you saved $1,652 each month for a rainy day or to put toward buying your first home someday. Now you're starting your own good times. Working can be fun if you have an open mind and a good attitude.

Maybe because of my rough upbringing and need for attention, I always excelled in work, and I loved the competition in it. As a young employee, work was like a sport in many ways. You are starting at the bottom, and there are other young employees starting at the bottom as well. Who is going to rise up to the challenge? Which one is going to get promoted first? You show up on time, you work hard, you're diligent in your work, and you try to be the best in your field. Go to your boss and ask for other tasks to do once you completed the ones you were given. You don't have to be a kiss-up. You just need to be the best at what you're doing. Once you get that promotion, set your goals on another.

Just like in sports, you want to make the team, then you want to be a starter, then you want to be the best on the team, and then the best in the league. You do it in fair play. You don't do it through cheating or deception. You do it with a team attitude in the spirit of competition. You're helping the company grow, you're pushing your coworkers, and you're learning the business as you compete.

Who wants to show up for work every day just looking for a paycheck? How boring is that? Unless you have been blessed to have millions of dollars handed to you, you should get used to the fact that you will be working for a long time. Make the most fun out of it you can. Meet people you work with. Talk to your coworkers about their interests or start a discussion about their families. You may have something in common.

If things are not working for you at this job, find one that will be better for you. Note: Never quit a job unless you have another one to go to. Remember, you don't have to work at a job that was like the machine shop job that I had. You have options. Change it, accept it, or leave. You could go to your bosses with helpful ways to make the working environment better for everyone. Maybe talk about better ways for the employees to communicate with the management. That would be changing it.

You should try your best to be upbeat and positive. Try staying focused on the competition and advancement. You could just find a way to deal with the issues the best you can, realizing things may not be so bad. That would be accepting it. Or you could start looking for another job, maybe a career change. Once you realize that you can't change anything and you won't accept things the way they are, then leave. Again, never leave a job without having a job to replace it.

Good times are ahead of you if you help create them. Making good decisions with thoughts on a long-term plan is best. Never look for the shortcut. I would like our younger generation to believe in their abilities to work hard and believe that by knowing they can work hard, they will make out just fine during their lifetime.

I remember this as if it were yesterday. When I was about to turn eighteen years old, I realized that I was going to be on my own soon. Like most kids, I did not have anyone I could lean on for a job, a loan, or advice. I knew that it was time for me to start making decisions on my own, and I would be the only one who would benefit or lose out because of those decisions. I decided to take an offer from San Francisco State to play football. It didn't work out, and I needed to make some new decisions. I decided that I was going to be the hardest worker I could be. Nobody would deny me of that.

I was feeling a little down on myself and wanting to blame someone for the lack of being supported or financially set up. I realized none of that mattered anymore. I was eighteen years old now, and I could start all over again. I could learn from the problems my stepfather made, and I could learn from the adults who came and went in my younger life who made the right decisions. I was going to start all over again, and this time I was in charge. I was not going to take any shortcuts. I had my ability to work hard, and I had my word, which is something that is very important also.

Your word is huge in life when you decide that you are going forward on your own. I have seen firsthand what happens to people when they don't pay their bills, and I have seen firsthand what happens when your credit rating is so low that no bank or credit card company will lend you money. You having bad credit is like somebody saying your word is no good. I take great pride in my word being good, and so should you. Stand behind what you say and never say something you can't stand behind.

I went out and got my first credit card from a department store, and I never missed a payment. I mean never. I once was down to 29 cents in my checking account after paying one of those payments, but I paid it, and I went without for a while, but my word stayed true. I said if you loaned me the money I would pay it back, and every month I did.

I've seen the landlord banging on our door wanting the rent. I've seen the utilities turned off because payment was not made. I saw my stepfather asking friends and family for loans because he could not get money from the bank. This is no way to live, and it is not necessary. Credit cards and bank loans and borrowing money from a friend is you saying, "I will take the money from you and I will pay it back under the terms that we agree to"; this is you putting your word on the fact you will pay it back. If you pay it back within the agreed-upon terms, your word become valuable. The next time you need the money, you will get it, and you pay that back and your word becomes even more valuable, and so on. Stay within whatever you are comfortable with when you use your word. If you promise to pay a debt, then pay the debt. Don't take on a debt if you can't pay it back. Very simple.

I was eighteen years old and working the drive-through counter at my job with the dry cleaners. This woman was a regular customer and was a very nice person. She drove a brand-new silver Corvette. She was probably in her late thirties at the time and looked very professional. She and I had polite small talk whenever she drove in, but I never asked what she did for a living.

A few months passed, and a friend of mine asked me if I wanted to buy his car from him. I really wanted this car. It was a 1975 Monte Carlo, black on black, electric sunroof, True Spokes rims, and it was super clean. The problem was I needed a loan. I could not afford his car. Even after selling my car, I would still need a bank loan.

We went together to a local Bank of America in town and asked for a loan officer. We were directed to my friend from the drive-through cleaners, the lady who drove the silver Corvette. This was awesome, I thought. I know this lady, and she seems to get along with me just fine at the cleaners. So we sat down. She was very gracious and helpful, as I thought she would be, until she explained to me that because of my "good but little credit," I would need a cosigner for this deal to get done.

I sank into my seat and looked at my friend and said, "We'll need to leave. This won't work." I thanked her for her time and said, "I'm sorry, but that I can't do."

She asked, "Why not? Can't you ask your parents or a relative to cosign for you?"

I told her I could not. I told her my stepfather had horrible credit, my mom was a stay-at-home mom, and I would not ask anyone else to do that. "If I can't get a loan myself, then I will have to wait." I told her if she could give me the loan, I would give her my word that I would pay it back, saying, "I will give you my personal promise that I will pay the loan back." Finally, I told her I did learn some things from my stepfather's money problems and his bad credit issues and that I'd never live like that. "You have my word on it", I said.

She stared at me for a few seconds and said, "Donnie, I have never given anybody a loan before based on their word. However, I have never met anybody who was so passionate about his word before either. You'll get the loan, and I know you will pay it back." Of course I did pay it back, never missing a payment. I hope you will learn as a young adult, being true to your word, being an outstanding employee, and becoming independent can be a lot of fun. Those traits will set you up for a life of good times.

No matter what hand in life you are dealt as a child, rich, poor, good athlete or bad, it really doesn't matter. Someday you'll be a legal adult, and that day you'll get to start all over. But this time, you'll be calling all the shots. There are no shortcuts, and you don't need them anyway.

I have been around coaches who would spend an enormous amount of time trying to find the new fandangle offense that will surprise everyone the next season or the great special teams tricks to grind out victory after victory. Some coaches would watch a college tape and not understand that some things just don't work in high school as they do in college. In college you hand-pick your players to fit in your system, in high school you get who signed up. So, trying new things is fine; you just have to know that it may not work.

There is no quick fix to having success. Working with a solid plan and developing your players is where you should be. The credit and the glory that you seek is there if you do everything right and have some patience. Success is something you want to last a long time, so take the time to get it there. Just like bad debt: It may have taken you years to get in that deep, so what makes you think you'll be out of it in two weeks by coming up with some shortcut? I don't think so. You'll have to put together a plan, you'll have to make some sacrifices, and you'll have to be patient. Then you'll be enjoying "The Good Times" once again.

16

Saving Our Programs

Our economy is facing some hard times these days, and everyone knows that cutbacks need to be made. There is plenty of waste in our local government that needs to be reevaluated first before we start looking at our high school sports programs as areas that need to be cut. I know firsthand that the high school sports programs will help kids a lot more than these administrators and government officials know. I also know that most high school administrators and government officials don't want to see these programs cut, yet they place them on the chopping block long before looking to cut other programs. Sometimes they use high school cutbacks as leverage for passing a parcel tax or as a decoy to cover a project they don't want to cut that is less important.

In any case, I say enough. Enough of our school's sports programs barely getting by. Enough of asking parents to pick up the shortfall again this year because there are not enough funds to support the program their child is participating in. Just like everything else our local government will ask us to do, we do.

If we have a water shortage, the local government will raise the water rates. And when the shortage is over, the rates stay the same because the government got used to that money coming in and they figure you got used to paying it. So the rates never return back down. Same with the power shortage, same with gasoline, and same with our schools.

Whether you are a Democrat or a Republican, I don't care. We have to stand up for the kids, and we have to stand up for what we want out of our administrators and politicians. There needs to be guidelines that they follow, and if they can't follow them, they don't get reelected. Plain and simple. They don't get to keep their jobs. Whether you are in a union-organized job or not, vote for what you believe is the best for our kids and their sports programs. Don't just vote the same way your union representatives ask you to vote, unless you agree with them that the same vote is best for our schools and athletic programs.

We need better teachers and more of them. We need sports programs, and we need better coaches and more of them as well. We need playing fields that don't have potholes in them. We need safe bleachers for people to sit on, scoreboards that work, and lights for our fields. We need locker rooms and classrooms without asbestos and lead-based paints. We need high schools that are state of the art, and I'll tell you why. Pride!

We need high school sports for many reasons. And if you have been paying attention to this book, you know how important sports were for me. There are thousands of kids like me out there, and they need a second chance at life too. I don't know where I would be if I did not have a sport to help distract me from some of my issues. I am afraid to think of what I may have done or what crime I may have committed without sports.

If a school physically shows pride by its very own appearance, then the kids will have pride in it. They will have pride in their school decades after they leave it. Teachers will have pride when they pull up in the morning in the parking lot, ready to go to work. They will have pride in the school when they walk down the halls in a well-maintained corridor that has fresh paint on the walls and ceilings. They see a beautiful school, happier kids, smiling coworkers, and pride everywhere.

It's been thirty years after high school for my friends and me, yet we still talk about how our school was better than our friends over at De Anza High School. We are just joking, of course, but we believe a lot of it, and they argue the other side because they had a nice school as well, and they took pride in it.

When you have pride in your school, you're more likely to go to school than you would if it was a depressing dump. A nice school loaded with pride that has good, positive teachers and has good, positive coaching will create better enrollment and better participation in the sports programs. We need the sports to stay in these communities.

The less-than-average student will get better grades when playing sports. They have to. If they don't carry at least a C average, they won't be able to play. This is a big incentive for the average student-athlete to work on their schoolwork. If they don't have a sport to keep their interest, then they may just drop out of school. Some kids come from homes that may have a single, working parent. These single, working parents may not have the time to sit by the child's side every night helping him or her with their homework. Sports will help them work harder at the schoolwork on their own. Without sports in high school, these would-be C students will become D or F students because of lack of interest.

We need to support our schools with our taxpayer's dollars and donations. We need to support our schools with our time and commitment. If your state doesn't have the money, then ask your local representatives for a list of all local government-funded programs and see if you can come up with some projects that can be eliminated in order to make room for our schools. We need to let our local politicians know that the schools and sports programs are no longer taking cuts. And if they can't figure out how to get it done, then they will be replaced in the next election.

We want good schools, and we want good adults running the school and sports programs. We are not accepting no for an answer.

Sports will be an incentive for them to keep the grades up, and it will teach them to work for something because the reward is right now in the moment, getting to participate in the sport. This may also be the only chance some of these kids will have to get into college. Without a sports scholarship, their parents won't be able to afford for them to go. Without the reassurance of college being paid for by their parents and knowing that there is no chance of a sports scholarship, they may give up on grades altogether. I think without sports you will have a lot more kids taking the General Educational Development (GED) test as opposed to sticking around and graduating. That is a shame. High school used to be so much better and fun to be a part of before local government and school administrators got carried away with budget cuts in sports.

Kids learn a lot about life's lessons through sports as well. They learn about teamwork. They learn about dedication and pride. Who will teach dedication and pride if not school sports? The local drug dealer? Kids will be taught development in their sports, which will help them with the transformation from high school sports to college sports. With good coaching, they will learn ethics and principles. If they are troubled from a personal problem at home, who do they talk to if not their coach?

Parent involvement at the school will dwindle to a minimum without sports. There would be no pride or confidence in the school system, and without pride and confidence in the system, why would anyone want to be a part of it? We all need to stand up and let our local administrators and politicians know that they need to do a better job because their lack of pride in their jobs isn't working for us.

Without sports in high school, we will also have a decline in community pride and support. They all fit together: your local high school, the local banks, the local grocery store, the bike shop, the yogurt shack, the newspaper, the pizza place, and the golf course. They all are a part of the community, and they all donate money year after year. With the decline of confidence in the school system and the lack of confidence in our local government, why would they continue to donate money? Why throw good money after bad? The more we give the administrators, the more they want.

I think it's time for them to cut their own pet projects and leave ours alone. Without sports, some kids will drop out of school, and our crime rate will rise. They may end up buying or selling drugs, as if we need more of that around. Pride will be lost in the community, in the school, and in the kids. We will see housing prices drop even more or at least take longer to rebound. People will sell their home and move their kids to areas that have better high school programs, and our homes' values will drop because of it. No family will want to move into an area that has lousy schools, higher crime, more drugs, and no pride.

We all need to stand up and let our officials know enough is enough and let them know we will have a zero tolerance plan going forward, meaning their jobs will be closely watched. We need to let them know that they work for us, and their number one duty is to do what we need done or step down.

Let's work with them. Let's help them the best we can. And if they feel they want to go in a different direction, let's help them get out of politics all together. After all, they did run their campaigns every election on the things they know you want, and when they get into office, they act like you're asking for something new. They said they understood our problems, and they said they could help. Well, start helping, politicians and administrators, or get out of our way.

Getting back to business, we as business owners need to build programs for our employees that will provide safety on the job. Sometimes, a new or unexpected situation will arise and that may require new programs to be created or some minor adjustments to programs that may already be in place. Never do we create programs just to create programs. By creating a weak or unnecessary program, employers may diminish the programs that they have currently in place, in the view of their employees.

Programs that are designed to give the employer more control over the employees, as opposed to programs designed for safety or better sales opportunities or programs that have been designed to improve the workplace, will never work. Programs like a Global Positioning System on the employees' vehicles, programs designed to rat out a coworker, programs that remove employees' privileges such as personal office phone time, these are just not realistic and will never be taken seriously by the employee. And besides, employees will waste even more time finding creative, sneaky ways to do it anyway.

If the employer implements too many programs, and if the employer implements controlling programs, their employees will not take any of them seriously, not even the important ones you need followed. The employees will become overwhelmed with too many programs and not be able to decide which ones are really important and which ones are not as important. They cannot follow them all.

Focus on the programs that are needed for bettering the company and the workplace environment. Implement as few of them as you can, and stay consistent with them. Changing programs every other week or forgetting that you have programs in place until a problem occurs is program suicide.

If you are the head coach of a youth football team and your players are being dropped off for practice late every day, then you have a problem. Practice cannot start on time when only half of the players are present. Hold a meeting with your players' parents, and let them know of your problem. Explain to them your solutions, and ask them if they have any ideas of their own. By giving the parents an opportunity to help resolve the problem, they will be more likely to help you follow the new program, besides the fact they have helped create the program and are now a part of the new program. They will understand its importance.

Getting employees involved will have the same results. Evaluate the problem, then have a solution in mind and present it to the employees. Let them know about the problem, give them an opportunity to help with the solution, and you'll see them getting behind you with the new program.

Understanding the depth of your problems will help you create programs that are important. Sports programs for local high schools are at the very top of the list for me. I would like everyone to know about this problem, and I would like everyone who is reading this book to get involved in their community and develop a program that will keep money in their schools for sports programs.

My wife and I are involved in a program that can help these school districts with their fundraising by having the parents purchase energy drinks and protein powders that are safe and nutritional for their kids. Some of the money from these purchases goes to the districts (not for profit) organization. As a business owner I like these types of programs because the people you are asking to give you money are getting something in return, and it's something they are buying already for their kids. These products work and are better for them as they are "White Listed" by the International Olympic Committee. Meaning no doping.

The district gets the residual money every month from every sport. Go to your web-browser and type in www.howellhealth.com to learn more about these type of programs for your district.

This is different than asking people to just give money ever year without a plan for next year. The business that gave $50,000.00 this year may be out of business next year, then who covers that money? The parents could be strapped for money or may have more than one kid playing a sport, should they pony up more than once? Can they be counted on every year?

If people get creative and more demanding of our elected officials, I think some positive solutions will rise to the top. We have to keep trying to find better ways to keep sports in play.

I welcome your thoughts on what you would like to do about it or what solutions you may have regarding a new program for keeping sports alive in high school. My solution would be putting more pressure on our elected officials and administrators with a zero tolerance for reelection. If you cannot get it done, then get out of the way.

In addition to putting pressure on the elected officials and administrators, I would like to see combined efforts from the school principal, the Booster Clubs, and a committee of parents who will work together with the head coaches to ensure our kids are getting the best efforts from all adults in keeping sports alive and fun.

I know there are many great head coaches and athletic directors out there in high school sports, so let's focus on helping them all stay in the game.

I'm sure the good ones won't have a problem with it. Some may even embrace it. Let's be there for them and let's find creative ways to bring in money for all the school sports. The importance of these program is to keep kids, pride, and sports in our high schools. Let's make sure our efforts are as good as our words.

E-mail me your thoughts at dwh322@comcast.net.

17

Stating the Obvious

There are times when you have to ask the question, why does anyone need to be reminded about ethics and principles? After all, that is what this book mostly is about, giving people awareness through my experiences. I have seen so many good people become tyrants as coaches, and they don't even realized it happened; you ask them what is wrong with them, why are they acting like this, and they reply, "You're right, I'm sorry to have lost control of myself." They don't realize how important it is to remember the reason they wanted to be a coach in the first place. Why do they get so wrapped up in winning that they forget their principles and become the type of coach they never liked? They wanted to be a part of the game and they wanted to help kids, is what they tell you. So why not go into it with a plan that will make it fun for everyone? Take into consideration the kids, the parents, the administrators, the fans, and the community. Put together a well-thought-out plan for creating fun for everyone and use common sense when a decision needs to be made. The games are being played because mothers and fathers want their kids to play football, they want their kids to be a part of a team, and they want it to be fun for the whole family. As a coach, you should have these thoughts in your head while putting together your plan for the team. You should have a plan that includes you having fun also. You should understand what type of coach you want to be, and you need to understand what type of assistants you will allow around the players and parents. You will need to hold a meeting with the parents to lay out a few ground rules with the kids in mind and offer areas where they can help and be a part of the team and the plan. Educate your assistant coaches in the areas you will need them to coach, allow them to offer some of their input, and if they are capable experienced coaches, then allow them to proceed in a way they would like; why not, if it's close to your plan and it's good for the kids? Inform every one of your coaches to remind themselves that when speaking to the kids, they should do it in a positive manner. Having a plan for success is planning for a successful season.

This also may be obvious but again needs to be said: as a parent you also have a role to play with the coaches and the players. It is not the place for you to be running around and second-guessing every decision the coach is making. Your role should be to get with the coach from the very beginning and ask him some questions like, what are your ethics and principles? Is there any way I can help out the program?

You could let the coach know some of the qualities that you have to offer, and he may find a place for you to help. Get to know the other parents on your team and get to know some of their insight as to how the team is progressing. Keep things positive when talking to the other parents, you are only asking them because you want to make sure the things that the coaches discussed with all of you from the first day are getting done.

There have been many times I've spoken to some friend years after a season was over and they would tell me how disappointed they were with a coach they had, and another person would say, "My son was on that team also and I didn't like him either." They would say that coach never kept his word about the kids' playing time or they would say the coaches were in the kids' faces all the time. However, neither of these parents spoke about an issue that may have been easily corrected had they gone to the coach at the time. The coach may have thought he was doing as he promised on that first day. He may have been focused on something else and the parents were afraid to speak up. The coach may have had a personal problem and never noticed himself screaming at the kids. Nothing changed for these parents and players because change was never mentioned or discussed with the coach.

If these parents had talked throughout the season, they may have gone to the coach in a positive manner and said, "Some of the kids are not getting the playing time that they should; you told us in the beginning of the season every kid would play a minimum of eight plays, that is not happening." The coach most likely will correct the problem if that is what he said. These parents could have put a stop to the yelling and screaming at the kids had they brought it to the attention of the coach. If the coach doesn't respond in a positive manner, then at least you have met someone (another parent) who will help you should you feel that going above the coach's head is needed. The point is to get to know the other parents and get to know how they feel about what is going on. Besides, you may find everything is going to plan and they are enjoying themselves. You may even meet a parent who you can split duties with in helping the team with snacks or dressing the field before a game, and along the way, you may find a new friend or two.

Assistant coaches have roles to play as well, and it's not just doing whatever the head coach says. When a head coach has a great program going, and it's been proven year after year, then yes, you can feel comfortable in the fact this experienced person is using his ethics and principles and now you have something fun going on here for everyone. However, you too should be listening on day one when the head coach gives his speech, and you need to make sure you believe in his message; if you don't believe in the message, then you need to get with the head coach in private and help correct the message. If he is unwilling to do so, then you may want to coach somewhere else. Why would you want your ethics and principles being confused with someone else's just because he is a head coach? You also should be coaching with a positive message for the kids to follow. Going into the season with the expectation of everyone having a good time might seem to be obvious, but unless everyone really works at it together, it will just be another year of frustration for the parents, the players, and yourself.

The same thing applies to business; it might sound obvious but we need to build a workplace where everyone can enjoy themselves. When your employees are happy and when they feel like they are a part of the company's plan and the course it is on, they work better. When they have a say in it, they perform better; when they feel like the company is committed to its ethics and principles, then they will lead it. The employees need to have stability, and they need to know you as the owner have a plan, one that includes the future and one that includes growth. As obvious as it might sound, they don't need a hypocritical, arrogant leader who looks to blame others when mistakes happen and sucks up all the credit when good things happen. Just stay supportive and positive with all your employees, and they will work hard and successfully for the company.

No one can say or predict that a company will fail one day just based on the fact that the company was never really run with good ethics and proper principles. But I have seen small companies become large companies, and after they became a large company, they got greedy and moved away from their business plans, and they took advantage of their employees and did lose it all once the economy slipped. They would use unethical practices because they were on top during a good economy and did not have the wits about them to plan for the day when the economy turned. They traded their ethics and their principles for personal gain, which came back to bite them when their top-level employees decided to jump ship as the company boat was taking on water. These types of company leaders showed a lack of loyalty to the employees, so the employees had no loyalty to the company when times got tough. Nobody really plans for the bottom to fall out, but not having a plan to treat people right during good times is really planning on being alone should the bottom fall out.

These kinds of company leaders didn't take into consideration that there are other people who run the departments, and they cannot run all the departments without the employees helping them. They could replace some of them, but that requires retraining people, and that's not productive, nor does it show loyalty. Spend the time up front with your employees and the company plan. Most employees really do want a place to work that is fun and productive and where they can grow and feel important. Most employees would like to work in a place that has a plan for them to succeed, and they would be willing to stay for many years to come. The longer they stay, the less you are teaching and the more productive they can become.

I think most employers start out wanting to be fair with their employees, but a few will lose that thought as time goes on and they become complacent and get richer. But most are very ethical and most have great principles, and that is why I always paid attention to the ones who have been around a long time, the ones who have been through good times and bad times before. I've learned a lot from those companies that have employees that have been with them for decades and would never think of leaving. These employees found a company that is working toward a common goal with them, and these companies have allowed them to take ownership in it as well. When times got tough, they worked through it with communication, and together the company leaders and the employees made cutbacks and tightened budgets together. If your employer allowed you and your coworkers to sit down with them and discuss some tough cut-back decision making, wouldn't you appreciate that? They would be (rightfully) seen as a company that is trying to be fair to everyone yet has a problem that needs to be fixed. The news may be bad but change is coming and you have a part in it. If a company uses team effort, has growth, and focuses on job security, then why on earth would anyone want to leave? It might be obvious to some, but unless you have a focused business plan that includes good ethics and good principles, you may find that greed and selfishness will work its way in, and that cannot be good for anyone.

As for the coaches running their own programs, try to remember that you are not alone, you have assistant coaches and parents there to help. They will be there in a minute should you need help. They also feel the problems you and the team may be going through, so they should be acknowledged and complimented from time to time. Don't be afraid the next time you're being interviewed by the newspaper to mention that your special teams coach did a great job or your defensive line coach really got the kids ready that week. Spread around some of the credit, and you'll find that there is still some left for you. Use your ethics and principles every day, coach with passion for the kids, and let the parents get involved so they too can get behind the program. Continue with the good ethics and principles throughout your career, whether you had a winning season or not. Focus on doing the right things for the kids; it's their sport and it's their time, and along with you, they and their parents should enjoy the whole experience. Taking the time to build a program right is in your best interest, because once in place and once it's successful, it will take on a life of its own, and when it does, you'll have the kids, the parents, and the community wanting to get behind it with you, and everyone will come out winners. It might sound obvious but winning is great, and we should all try our best to win, but it's not everything.

Explanation Sheet

Please take the time to review the Parent Cheat Sheet and the Seasonal Program Contract in the pages to follow. These items are intended to help the coaches and parents plan for a successful youth sports season. Everyone starts out with good intentions and hopes for the best, and I'm sure they believe that. However, I think putting those hopes to ink will get all parties trying a little harder.

These are sample versions that can and should be revised to better fit your youth sport and your individual needs.

The Parent Cheat Sheet is designed to help you ask questions when being introduced to your new head coach. You may have other questions or more direct questions; feel free to include or delete them as you look to fulfill your needs. Please keep in mind the format is not designed for you to be disrespectful or inappropriate. Stay positive and supportive but get your questions answered.

The Seasonal Program Contract is a designed program that the coach and the parents should work through. This program will only work if both parties have a say in it. This program needs to be fair to all, and the commitments need to be clear and simple. Avoid making these contracts complicated. We are really looking to keep fair play and sportsmanship in the overall program.

Parent Cheat Sheet

Standard first-day questions you may want to ask your new head coach:

1.) Do you coach with ethics and principles? And if you do, could you explain them to us?

2.) How will you select your assistant coaches, and will they be required to follow your same ethics and principles?

3.) Will every kid have an opportunity to compete at all positions, or have you preselected some players already?

4.) If willing, can parents participate in your program, and if so, where would you see them helping?

5.) Will you describe what a typical practice day is like?

6.) If number 5 is not completely explained, then ask, How much time will be dedicated to conditioning and running laps every day as opposed to teaching football?

7.) What is your work schedule like, and will you be able to be at all scheduled practices and games, or do you have an alternate plan?

8.) As parents, we want the season to be as successful as you do, so how can we help?

9.) Will all of our kids be ready to advance to the next level by the end of this season? If so, how?

10.) How much screaming and yelling by your coaching staff is allowed?

11.) Are you willing to sign a Seasonal Program Contract with us?

Seasonal Program Contract

This is the team seasonal contract to be reviewed and agreed upon by the head coach, parents, and players. This written agreement is put into place as a guideline for all parties to have a fun and successful sports season. Please review the following information and discuss any differences or changes you may feel need revising. Once agreed to and signed by all parties, you may all begin your fun-filled season.

HEAD COACH

I hereby agree to coach these kids to the best of my abilities. I will coach with the intent to create a learning environment for these kids. I will coach with the best modern technical information I can get. I will insure safety to the best of my abilities. I will hand-select my assistant coaches through an interviewing process that I develop. The interviewing process will include questions on football knowledge, time they are willing to donate, their commitment to the entire season, their ethics and principles, and their goal for the kids. I further agree not to allow any assistant coaches to be involved with the program if they do not meet these minimum requirements.

I will do my best to put the kids in a position to win at all times and will teach them to win with respect. I will furthermore teach them to lose with respect, should they come out short on the scoreboard. My coaching staff and I will do our best to make these young players better people, better students, and better players by season's end.

Under my program, every kid will have the same opportunities as the next. Race, religion, sex, or physical abilities will not affect their chances. No kid will receive special treatment simply because of a parent's position on the team or in the community. All kids will have the right to compete fairly for all positions on the team.

Any person or parent willing to participate in the program, who meets the above requirements, will have an opportunity to help. I will do my best to find a position for this qualified person. I cannot guarantee the position they may seek, but I will find something that will make them feel welcomed and needed.

PARENTS

I hereby agree to be supportive to the coaching staff. I will offer my time and services to help the program in any way (within reason) as asked by the head coach. I will take time to meet and get to know the other parents and the coaching staff. I will have my kid at all scheduled events on time. I promise never to show up with my kid late or absent without at least a phone call to the head coach. If my personal time is limited, I will at a minimum provide the head coach with a schedule of times that I may be able to assist.

I promise never to scream or yell from the stands. To the best of my abilities, I will try and be a role model fan when I'm in the stands during a game or on the sidelines at practice. Should I have a problem with the head coach or one of his assistants, I promise to go to the head coach first and ask for a private meeting with the head coach or the assistant coach. I further promise to discuss any problems in a mature and adult way.

I promise never to judge the coaching staff solely based on if the team wins or loses. I understand that if the coaching staff is committed to teaching and being fair to all kids, and the coaching staff is using good ethics and principles, we are all winning anyway. I promise to do my part in making this season a positive fun environment for everyone.

PLAYER

I promise to be on time to all scheduled events. I promise to maintain good grades while in school. I promise to obey my parents, my teachers, and my coaches. I promise to speak with respect to my parents, my teachers, and my coaches. I promise to work hard at my sport. I promise to be a good teammate and a good sportsman at all times. I promise to help the kids younger than me be successful, and I promise to support my teammates at all times. If I am having a tough day, I promise to speak to my parents or my coach about it in order not to take out my frustrations on the team. I will be a good teammate, and I will show good sportsmanship at all times.

Coach_____

Parents_____

Player_____

CPSIA information can be obtained at www.ICGtesting.com
Printed in the USA
LVOW061223230112

265161LV00001B/34/P